HAUNTED RESTAURANTS and BARS of NEW MEXICO

HAUNTED RESTAURANTS and BARS of NEW MEXICO

DONNA BLAKE BIRCHELL

Published by Haunted America
A division of The History Press
An imprint of Arcadia Publishing
Charleston, SC
www.historypress.com

Copyright © 2026 by Donna Blake Birchell
All rights reserved

All photos courtesy of the author.

First published 2026

Manufactured in the United States

ISBN 9781467158770

Library of Congress Control Number applied for.

Notice: The information in this book is true and complete to the best of our knowledge. It is offered without guarantee on the part of the author or The History Press. The author and The History Press disclaim all liability in connection with the use of this book.

All rights reserved. No part of this book may be reproduced or transmitted in any form whatsoever without prior written permission from the publisher except in the case of brief quotations embodied in critical articles and reviews.

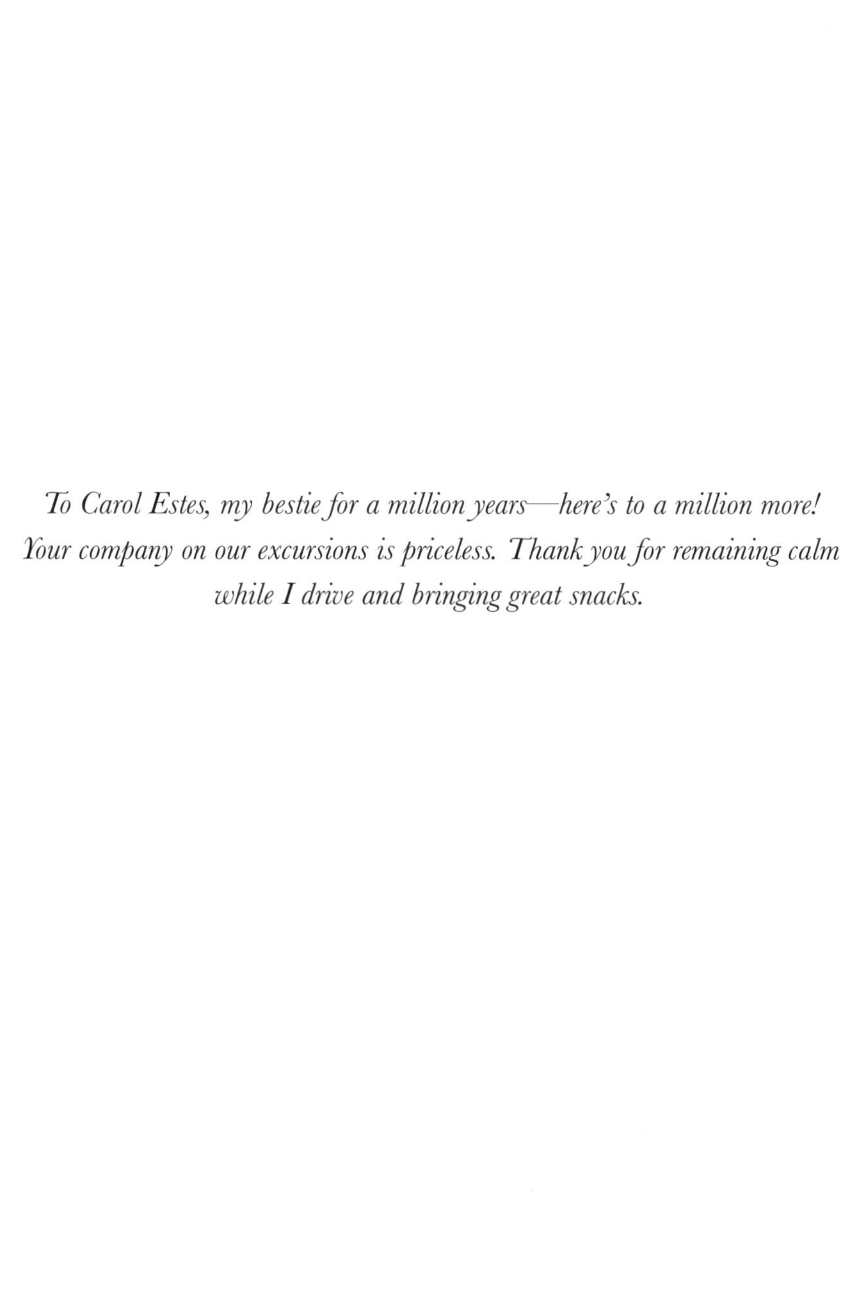

To Carol Estes, my bestie for a million years—here's to a million more! Your company on our excursions is priceless. Thank you for remaining calm while I drive and bringing great snacks.

CONTENTS

Acknowledgements

To my dear friend Samantha Villa Hardin, who started this whole ball rolling and gave me the extra boost to continue this great journey: I am forever in your debt.

To my entire family, old and new: I send you all my love and thank you from the bottom of my heart always for your support and being proud of this old woman. I cannot believe how blessed I am to have you all in my life.

To Carol and Richard Estes, who always have my back: I can't thank you enough for fifty-plus years of friendship.

To Jesse Herron, owner of the Painted Lady Bed & Brew, who came to my rescue once again: Thank you for all your great help.

To all those of you who relayed your ghostly experiences: I am forever grateful.

To the wonderful restaurants and bars included in this tome who continue to serve some of the best food and libations in the world to the citizens and visitors of the great state of New Mexico. Your efforts are greatly appreciated—and needed! You are keeping New Mexico history and traditions alive.

To my awesome editor, Laurie Krill, for all your guidance and patience: many thanks.

INTRODUCTION

New Mexico has been known by a couple of names since statehood in 1912, starting with the Sunshine State, which Florida has now adopted; it is now Land of Enchantment. This is a state of multiple diversities and cultures; each section of the state has its own mindset and beliefs. The diversity that makes up the fabric of this great state comes from the ability of many cultures to coexist in peace. Although it was not always this way in the past, it is good to see harmony today.

Vast turquoise skies, rugged mountain ranges, open plains, sagebrush-filled deserts, and natural wonders abound along the byways of this state. The scenery can change completely within a couple of highway miles, but no matter where you go, you will always see beauty, you just may have to look a little harder in some areas.

One of the biggest attractions of New Mexico is its food. As a highly agricultural state, New Mexico is most famous for its *chiles verdes*, or green chiles, grown primarily in the Mesilla Valley of the southwestern portion of the state. The tiny town of Hatch has become the "Green Chile Capitol of the World." Every August, the chile roasters come out of storage and adorn the porticos and sidewalks of every grocery store in the state while permeating the countryside with the official state aroma: roasted green chile. The only aroma that may beat this is the smell of a rain shower on the desert sagebrush.

Many New Mexico dishes include the green chile in one form or the other. There is even a wine made from both red and green chiles, which is

Hatch, New Mexico, is the Chile Capitol of the World—and for good reason, since it is surrounded by many fields of delectable green chiles.

an acquired taste for some. This author thinks that the red chile wine would make a wonderful marinade for beef or pork. Each section of New Mexico has its own distinct cuisine style, and all are equally delicious.

Northeastern New Mexico is highly influenced by the Spanish and Indigenous cultures; therefore, corn, squash, and beans are widely used, and red chile is the favored sauce. Northwestern New Mexico is influenced by the Navajo Nation and cowboy cultures that are more prevalent in the area, so dishes using frybread, steak, trout, and mutton are found in this region. Southwestern New Mexico is influenced by the Mexican and Native cultures, and although many of the dishes are the same as in other parts of the state, it is the green chile that rules as the choice of sauce. Southeastern New Mexico is mainly influenced by Mexican culture, but there is a heavy inspiration taken from nearby Texas for steak-and-potato-type meals as well. Central New Mexico is the melting pot of all cultures; Albuquerque, the largest city in New Mexico, is included in this region, and you will be able to find just about every type of food imaginable within the city limits.

Food is extremely important to the citizens of New Mexico and its visitors. Included in the *New Mexico Blue Book*, published annually by the Office of the Secretary of State, which is brimming with facts and statistics about New Mexico, is a list of the "officials" of the state. For example, the official cookie of New Mexico is the biscochito, which is a favorite at Christmastime, and the official question of the state is "Red or Green?," which refers to which type of chile sauce you want on your food. The official vegetables are the chile and the pinto bean. The official tree, the piñon, produces a nut that is used in many northern New Mexican dishes. In January 2023, a new "official" was added to the long list: the "official aroma of New Mexico," roasted green chile. Even the petals of the official state flower, the yucca, are edible and can be quite delicious when prepared correctly.

You may notice that some of the restaurants and bars included in this volume are connected to hotels, which are also reported to be haunted. A few of these were featured in my *Haunted Hotels and Ghostly Getaways* book as well, but new information has been added since that book was first published in 2018. Please feel free to use both as your haunted guides to New Mexico. You will also notice there are many references to a building, church, house, etc. being the "oldest." It might be fun for the reader to use these references as an Easter egg hunt of sorts—I guarantee you will find quite a few.

It's been asked many times why New Mexico has so many hauntings, and a theory has formed: Due to the over ten thousand known volcanos located in New Mexico, the state is a high-energy, high-vibrational land formed in great violence. Everyone and everything are forms of energy that react to their surroundings, and when people die violently, they are sometimes not aware of what happened to them and continue just beyond the veil in a different energy plane, trapped by the turbulent energy fields found in Land of Enchantment.

According to researcher, author, and investigator Cody Polston, there are five types of ghosts. The most common is the postmortem, which is the spirit of a person recently deceased who returns temporarily to say goodbye. The second is a crisis apparition, which can sometimes be called a premotion—in other words, visions of foreboding events. The third is called a bystander ghost, a personal spirit that follows a person throughout their life and can sometimes be mistaken for a psychotic episode. Fourth are hauntings, which is the phenomenon most think they experience: visitations or inhabitations by a ghost or spirit. The last is the most frightening: poltergeists, which were popularized by the movie of the same name, bring a certain amount of fear to most people's minds—but are defined merely as "noisy ghosts," from the German derivative. Polston states, "While hauntings tend to stretch over years or even centuries, poltergeist activity often lasts only a few months. And unlike most ghosts, poltergeists often focus their energy on a particular person, rather than a place."

Like most ghost stories, the ones in this book are based on stories passed down over the years or on eyewitness accounts, which have the tendency to change with each telling. True or not, they are all for entertainment purposes. Some tales are very well documented, while others are not. No matter what your beliefs, all I ask is that you read these spectral tales with an open mind and a light heart. If you enjoy the paranormal and want to get your heart pumping a bit faster, please use this book as a guide to find the well-known and lesser known reportedly haunted restaurants and bars of Land of Enchantment. Please patronize these establishments, have a great meal and spirits, and make up your own mind about the validity of the stories. You never know what or who you will find!

CHAPTER 1
NORTHEAST REGION

SANTA FE

Dubbed the City Different, New Mexico's capital city, Santa Fe, is also known as the oldest capital city in the United States; it also contains what is said to be the oldest house and church in the United States within its city limits. Indigenous people lived in this region for thousands of years before the Spanish Entrada of 1598 with Don Juan Oñate at the helm. This ancient city seems to lure free thinkers, artists, and intellectuals to live within its sunbaked adobe walls. As the stomping grounds for such notables as Georgia O'Keeffe, D.H. Lawrence, and, more recently, the late great actors Val Kilmer and Gene Hackman, Santa Fe has something for everyone—if you know where to look.

The blending of Indigenous, Spanish, Mexican, and Anglo cultures has formed a city full of wonderments, mysteries, and great food. The Santa Fe–style architecture, which features flat-roofed, thick-walled adobe structures as well as the Territorial-style buildings scattered in for good measure are a dream for those who love southwestern architecture and history. You may walk by without noticing, but at 106 Palace Avenue on the Plaza is the infamous starting point for the scientists who worked at nearby Los Alamos during the Manhattan Project, building the atom bomb. These scientists were not given a clue about where they would be working as it was a completely covert operation.

Left: You never know what you'll find in Santa Fe's eclectic art scene. You can be certain every street will be colorful as you stroll along.

Opposite: San Miguel Church, known as the oldest church, built in the United States, is graced with a hand-carved altar screen thought to be from 1798.

No trip to Santa Fe would be complete without a visit to the Loretto Chapel, home of the awe-inspiring miraculous spiral staircase and Bishop Lamy's St. Francis Cathedral, which dominates the Santa Fe Plaza landscape. Shops of every description are available for you to enjoy. Some of the finest examples of Native American jewelry are on display for purchase in the plaza shops and along the Palace of the Governors portico; these pieces are truly treasures and heirlooms.

During your ghost-hunting adventures, please take some time to visit Canyon Road, which is chock-full of world-renowned art and sculpture. Walking along this narrow road lined with historical adobe shops and galleries, decorated with small gardens of lavender and hollyhocks, you'll feel like you have stepped into a southwestern fantasyland. The variety of artwork and galleries will take your breath away or make you stop in wonder as you encounter original works from some of the world's most famous artists available for your close viewing.

Just know, and be prepared: Centuries ago, the tradition was to bury young members of the family who passed away under the brick or Saltillo tile floors

of the family home—homes that are now shops and galleries—rather than in the cemeteries. Priests and clergy members were often buried under the altar floors as well. This is why Santa Fe prides itself on its strict preservation of its historical buildings as sacred sites.

You will find that Santa Fe is not just a city but a complete experience.

INN AND SPA AT LORETTO/LUMINARIA 211 OLD SANTA FE TRAIL

One of the most stunning and most photographed properties in the heart of historical Santa Fe, the Inn and Spa at Loretto provides the true ambiance of Santa Fe style and grace. One of New Mexico's most beloved soups is served at the Luminaria as their signature dish: tortilla soup. Said to be good for the soul, this soup is made in many different varieties but is always delicious. The cuisine is locally sourced and organic for your culinary pleasure.

In honor of resident spirit Sister George, the Luminaria's lounge has a special drink named for her: the Smoking Nun. This concoction is made with Knob Creek rye whiskey, muddled orange, brandied cherry, Hennessy VSOP, Grand Marnier, and Regans' Orange Bitters, and lightly infused with smoke, and it is a must-have when visiting the inn. Be sure to cheers Sister George.

The 136-room hotel is the home of the only penthouse suite in Santa Fe. This exquisite suite features 360-degree views of the city from its five outdoor balconies, which makes it the most desired destination in Santa Fe, especially by celebrities. Be warned, this room also comes with a hefty room rate, so be prepared to spend an average of one month's apartment rent on one night's stay. This historic hotel is within walking distance of the Plaza, museums, and unique shops—and yes, it is dog friendly as well.

All the rooms are exquisitely decorated in a mixture of southwestern heritage and cultural styles of New Mexico. Wood-beamed ceilings convey a rustic charm to the luxury spa hotel as well as the oversized supple leather couches placed in front of an inviting roaring fire in the massive fireplace in the Luminaria bar. The white plaster walls provide a perfect backdrop for the world-class paintings that grace them. This is traditional New Mexico at its finest. Each room is equipped with a minibar and personal oxygen tanks to help guests should they experience any high-altitude sickness. Be sure to book a day at the spa while staying at the inn for a fabulous day of relaxation and pampering.

A must-see attraction connected to the Inn and Spa at Loretto is the world-famous French Gothic Revival–style Loretto Chapel, home to the miraculous spiral staircase. Legend states that in the 1850s, the architect of the chapel passed away before a staircase to the choir loft could be completed, leaving the nuns no access to this area, which was nearly twenty feet above them. After the nuns prayed novenas to Saint Joseph for nine days to find someone to build this staircase, a man named Joseph with a

It's considered the most photographed hotel in the state, and you can certainly see why when you approach the stunning Inn and Spa at Loretto.

tool-laden burro arrived and said he could complete the job, but he must be left alone. When the beautiful spiral staircase was completed three months later, Joseph and his burro disappeared as quickly as he appeared, leaving the nuns to wonder if they owed a bill at the local lumberyard. The answer

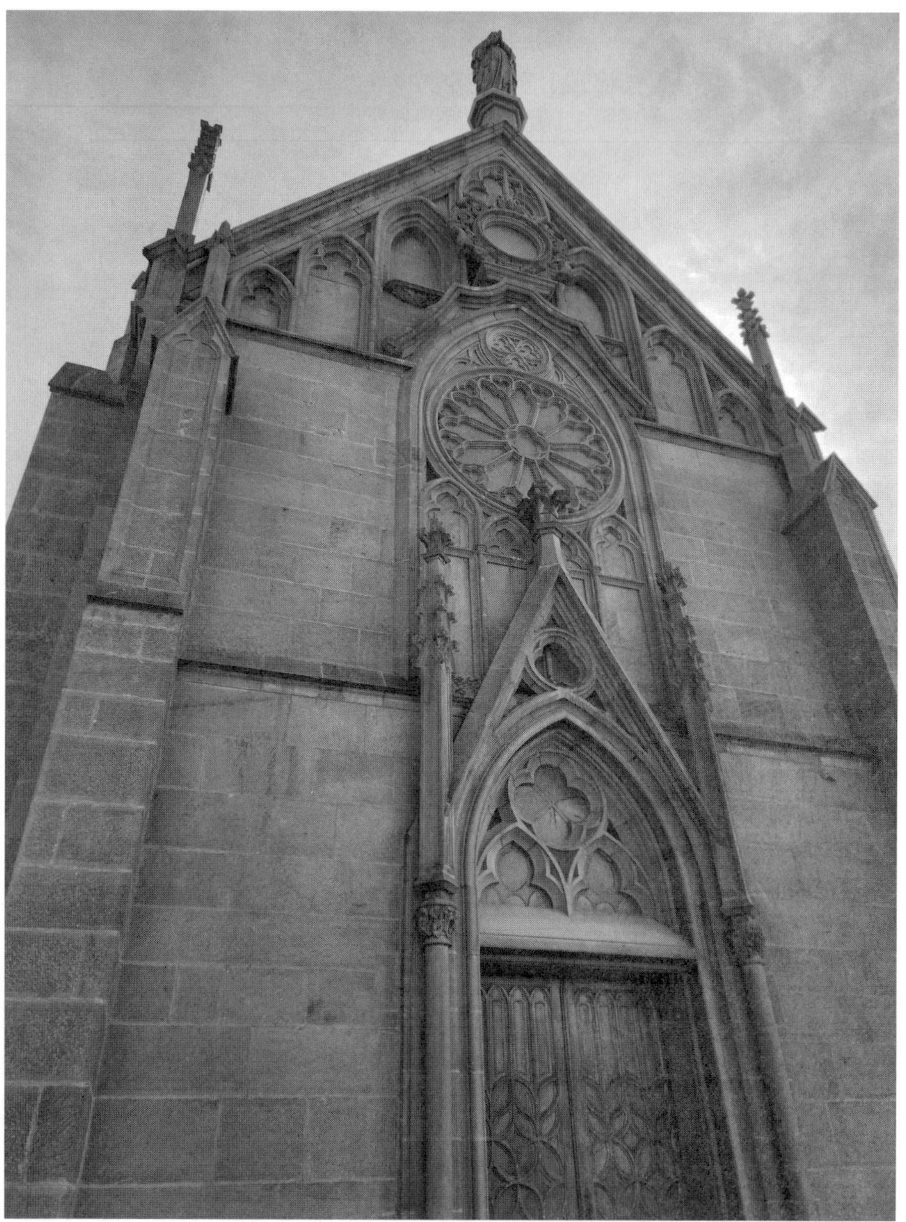

Loretto Chapel is home of the miraculous staircase thought to have been built by Saint Joseph himself for the nuns who prayed for him.

was no; Joseph had not purchased any wood or supplies from the store. On further inspection, the staircase was found to have been built without nails, only wooden pegs, and from wood not native to the area. The construction of the staircase still baffles architects and engineers today—but the nuns know it was a gift from God.

Haunted Tales

Sister George, the Cigar-Smoking Nun, who has been described as looking like she could be the sister of the late singer John Denver, is the biggest legend of this Santa Fe hotel. Sister George, who belonged to the Order of the Sisters of Loretto, walked to the beat of her own drum in life—and, apparently, in death as well. Sister George was a parochial woodworking teacher from 1853 to 1968 for the Loretto Academy, a Catholic girl's school that used to be housed in the current hotel; she passed away in 1976. When you smell the distinctive odor of burning cigars in the empty restaurant and hallways, you know you are in the good Sister's presence.

Staff members have reported receiving mysterious phone calls in the middle of the night originating from the fourth floor of the hotel—which was closed at the time the calls were made. This is significant since Sister George was reportedly fond of technology. When the concierge answers the calls, they are greeted with the familiar sound of answering machine music.

Guests have also reported feeling a hand placed on their shoulders after they smelled the smoke, as if they were being guided gently down the hallway. Adding to the mystique, hallway lights are known to flicker independently of the switches.

The inn offers a Ghost Walker's Package in honor of its spirit and the many others who call the City Different home. This package includes a one-night stay, a flashlight, a map, and a copy of the book *Santa Fe Ghosts* by Susan Blumenthal (which was a source for this book as well) to guide your way—if you're brave enough.

The Three Sisters Boutique, located in the hotel, has reported strange occurrences as well. The owners reported they would discover an extra ten dollars in the till each morning, which they took as a blessing from the good nun. Cigar smoke has also been smelled in the store, and orbs and lights have been seen turning off and on independently. Even the levitation of heavy clothing racks has been witnessed by the boutique staff.

LA FONDA ON THE PLAZA/LA PLAZUELA/LA TERRAZA 100 E. SAN FRANCISCO STREET

One of the oldest hotels in New Mexico, La Fonda on the Plaza was the destination for many travelers at the end of the Santa Fe Trail as well as the site of Santa Fe's first inn. The founder of the Santa Fe Trail, Captain William Becknell, and his party found their way to La Fonda on their first trek across country to establish the famed trail. It is also written that La Fonda (or, as it was known then, the Exchange Hotel), being one of the oldest and quite likely the largest buildings in Santa Fe during the 1600s, was used as a spot to perform hangings for the first six decade of its existence.

Many notables such as Wyatt Earp, Clay Allison, and Doc Holliday are said to have crossed the hotel's threshold during its long history. In the 1930s, the hotel was proud to claim, "All the world passes through our lobby." Although it was not then quite the place of grandeur seen today, La Fonda was a wild place and the site of many gruesome happenings, which has led to the idea that the hotel and bar are quite haunted.

There has been a hotel at the location of La Fonda on the Plaza since 1607, making this the oldest hotel corner in the country.

The magnificent structure you can visit today was built in 1922 and leased to the Fred Harvey Company. It was there that the Harvey House began in New Mexico. Harvey was a huge supporter of the local Native tribes and Spanish culture and would bring artisans in to display and sell their works to the guests. Tours, called Harvey Detours to La Fonda, were developed and were instrumental in introducing the world to the culture of Land of Enchantment. This hotel soon became a favorite destination for writers, politicians, and socialites from all over the world and is a prime example of Santa Fe elegance and architecture.

This historic hotel site—which is even rumored to have employed the young William H. Bonney, also known as Billy the Kid, as a busboy while he and his family lived in Santa Fe for a short time—offers ghost tour packages to entice the adventurous to explore the rich ghostly history of the capital city.

Haunted Tales

Videotaped accounts by New Mexico author Cody Polston of the various ghosts experienced in La Fonda on the Plaza by staff members and visitors can be found online in support of the following stories. Polston gives good arguments for the validity/or lack thereof these tales, stating that some cannot be backed up with actual historical records but have existed and been told for many years and new ones are added each year, making for good entertainment.

In 1857, a gambler was seized by a lynch mob and hanged in the backyard of the hotel. This yard has since been turned into the home of La Plazuela restaurant, and patrons of the eatery have reported seeing an image of a man hanging from the center beam.

Another tale connected to La Plazuela tells of a businessman who drank far too much and gambled away his company's fortune in a card game. The gentleman was so distraught that he ran to the inner courtyard (once located in the center of the restaurant) and threw himself in headfirst out of desperation. Reports of a ghostly figure seen walking in the center of the restaurant and jumping onto the floor are common. Wandering specters are also witnessed in the Santa Fe Room of La Terraza, a restaurant on the east side of the hotel's third floor.

Artwork, murals, and sculptures grace the lobby and hallways of La Fonda on the Plaza. Many of the works there rival the best in the surrounding galleries.

Ten years after the gambler was hanged, in 1867, Chief Justice of the Territorial Supreme Court John P. Slough was shot in the hotel lobby after a heated argument with Captain Rynerson, sparked when the judge insulted the captain. Rynerson was taken to court but was acquitted. Slough's ghost, clad in his signature black trench coat, still wanders the halls with heavy footsteps.

The lobby, Room 510, the basement, and the elevator of La Fonda are said to be haunted by a tragic young bride who was murdered on her wedding night in that room by an ex-lover. Another story of newlyweds' states that a groom went to the bar after the wedding, drank too much, and got into an argument with a bar patron that led him to be shot in the back while ascending the stairs to his room. Seeing her dead groom, the distraught bride is said to have shot herself on the staircase beside him.

A Santa Fe politician reportedly found his wife with another man at the hotel. The man was killed by the politician, but it was he who ended up hanged in the courtyard (now La Plazuela).

A Texas cowboy came to Santa Fe to avenge the death of a friend in the hotel bar. He proceeded to shoot two people before he was stopped and placed at the end of the noose in the hanging tree in the courtyard. This avenger can be found at the hotel bar between the hours of two and three o'clock in the morning and is often seen in the company of a ghostly bartender.

In the La Fiesta Lounge, a special drink is served in honor of the resident specters. Other than the ghostly residents of the hotel, visitors can also experience the spectral possibility of seeing Civil War soldiers on the property due to the proximity to the original Fort Marcy barracks.

LA POSADA HOTEL
330 E. PALACE AVENUE

Fashioned from what once was a magnificent 1882 Victorian mansion owned by Santa Fe Trail merchant Abraham Staab and his wife, Julia, La Posada Hotel is situated on six acres of prime Santa Fe real estate in the heart of the capital city. Surrounded by adobe walls, fountains, and high desert foliage, La Posada Hotel today bears little resemblance to the original three-story brick French Second Empire–style Victorian mansion until you arrive inside the lobby.

To the right of the check-in lobby area stand the concrete steps to the original glass and brass front doors, followed by the grand entry and staircase leading to what was once the primary Staab residence. On this spot, ghost tours are conducted where local "ghostorians" (yes, this is a made-up word) tell tales of the tragic Julia Staab, which we will also convey in a moment. According to the hotel's website, "The hotel embraces its haunted reputation, offering history tours that include tales of Julia and other ghostly encounters." Be sure to pick up some of their exclusive lotions and soaps from the lobby store while checking in; they are pure luxury.

As a newly established merchant and major supply contractor for the United States Army in the Santa Fe area, Abraham Staab worked diligently to grow his fortune so he could build a magnificent home, hoping to entice his wife, Julia, to follow him in his dream to live in the New Mexico Territory. Julia agreed, although she was not impressed by the dirty streets and adobe architecture that surrounded her newly built home.

The third floor of the Staab home was a grand ballroom in which Julia threw galas to show off the opulence of her home with great pride. The Staabs truly needed a lot of space to raise their six children. The Staabs' life was described as a fairy tale until the death of their seventh child, a son, shortly after his birth and several miscarriages.

Julia dove into an unconsolable depression; her beautiful black hair is said to have turned pure white. Tragically, Julia was to experience more heartache as several more unsuccessful pregnancies followed, sending the young mother over the edge in her grief. Unable to control her grief, Julia became a hermit and locked herself away in her room for the rest of her life. Julia passed away at the age of fifty-two in 1886, after many stated she became insane.

The surviving Staab children remained in the family home until they began their own lives. One can imagine this must have not been an easy childhood after their mother's depression and death. Abraham Staab passed away in 1913, after witnessing the destruction of Julia's beloved ballroom in a fire in the early 1900s.

The property did not switch to new owners until 1930, when it was sold to R.H. and Eulalia Nason, who turned the sprawling property into a hotel. It was the Nasons who built the Pueblo Revival style casitas around the existing Staab mansion and carriage house, naming their new dream La Posada—*posada* translates to "inn" or "resting place." The property lives up to its name, as the appointments of the rooms are spot-on and provide the guests with everything needed for a relaxing stay.

Two blocks from the Santa Fe Plaza sits La Posada, which was once a private residence. The adobe building of today encompasses the home.

Over the years, La Posada Hotel has been a generous host to the art and literary communities as schools and seminars have been conducted on its beautiful grounds. Despite Julia's tragic story, La Posada is such a romantic setting that it is a sought-after location for Valentine's Day lovers—and sometimes the Santa Fe weather will cooperate to provide a blanket of fallen snow to give you another good excuse (as if you needed more) to cuddle in front of the room fireplaces.

La Posada's lounge features tequila tasting every Monday and is conveniently located downtown, so it is within walking distance of many of Santa Fe's most treasured attractions. If you have time, book a spa day at La Posada, which will leave you feeling rejuvenated and refreshed.

Haunted Tales

Julia Staab, a beautiful young mother of six, loved her gorgeous home—so much so, many state, that she has never left its walls, even in death. Staff reports of Julia's continued presence began in the 1970s, when the late-night

Julia Staab's husband, Abraham, built a magnificent home for his bride, where the couple lived with their seven children. Julia may have never left.

cleaning crew stated they saw a "beautifully dressed translucent woman" standing near a fireplace. Rumors state that when a security guard for the property saw the same image later, he "took off running" since it frightened him so much. Guests report seeing Julia sitting in one of the armchairs in the lobby area—which was the front porch of her former home. The spirit tends to vanish soon after discovery, leaving the viewer to wonder if they really saw the ghostly image or not.

Located on the property is Julia's Spirited Restaurant and Bar, dedicated to former owner Julia Staab. It may be that Julia is not too happy to have a liquor establishment in her home as bartenders say they witnessed barware fly off the shelves, one piece at a time, crashing on the floor during a particularly busy night. On this same night, the bar's gas fireplace turned on and off without the benefit of human interaction, and the senior waitstaff began to drop heavy drink-laden trays continually during the night. Each reported they had the sensation of someone pushing the trays up from underneath.

A crying woman has been seen sitting on a stool in the corner of the bar dressed in period clothes. Guests and staff have determined that this is the ghost of Julia herself, still mourning the death of her child. Room 101, Julia's Suite, and Rose Suite seem to be favorite hangout spots for the spectral lady. The same image has been reported at Julia's final resting place in the nearby Fairview Cemetery where she and Abraham are buried, surrounded by some of their children.

To round out the spooky meter, there have been reports of books flying off bookshelves in the hotel lobby, and footsteps have been heard in the guest suites.

DRURY PLAZA/MASTERPIECE GRILL
828 PASEO DE PERALTO

Once the St. Vincent Hospital in the heart of Santa Fe, the renovated Drury Plaza sits adjacent to the stately St. Francis Cathedral, which is the largest landmark in the capital city, built between 1869 and 1886. Bishop Jean Baptiste Lamy used building on this site as a seminary, and it became known as the Old Seminary. In 1865, the bishop sold this building to the Sisters of Charity for use as a hospital. The hospital was in use from 1865 until the mid-1950s, when the nuns ran out of room and the need for another hospital became evident.

Famed architect John Gaw Meem (who is said to be responsible for the Santa Fe/Territorial style of architecture) drew up the plans for the new hospital—the same building in which the Drury Plaza is located—which served as St. Vincent's Hospital for the next twenty years, until 1977. Once

Striking Territorial architecture sets the Drury Inn apart from the surrounding adobe structures, but it melts into the historic setting perfectly behind its ornate iron gates.

a new St. Vincent's Hospital was built, the building became home to several offices for the New Mexico Department of Cultural Affairs and the New Mexico Film Commission. The location also served as a movie set for *Holiday in Santa Fe*, starring Mario Lopez and Emeraude Toubia, in 2021.

In 2007, the office building was purchased by the Drury Hotel chain and converted to the Drury Plaza Hotel we see today—but only after much restoration since it had become derelict. Archaeologists hired to study the history of the building site were able to uncover evidence of the original Sisters of Charity building foundations. While preserving the historic value of the property, the hotel added a restaurant, private terraces, and parking spaces to better serve its clients.

Haunted Tales

As the Drury Plaza started life a hospital, it has seen much tragedy during its existence since 1853. Hospitals and former hospitals are notorious for being hubs for paranormal activity.

Room 311 was where a small boy died as the result of a car accident; his agonizing cries were heard clearly after his death, so much so that the nurses sealed off his room. Activity reports from the Drury Plaza Hotel include guests experiencing the sensation of being touched even though no one is around and hearing loud banging noises coming from empty rooms and the sounds of footfalls in the hallways as though someone is running—and, unsurprisingly, voices in the basement.

The strange activity at the Drury Plaza is sometimes attributed to residuals connected to the site once being a church that was destroyed during the Pueblo Revolt of 1680. During this uprising, over four hundred Spanish settlers were brutally killed in the Santa Fe area, causing the few survivors to flee south along the Rio Grande for their lives. Those remaining met tragic ends, leading to the numerous, sometimes horrific, tales of apparitions in Santa Fe.

GERONIMO RESTAURANT 724 CANYON ROAD

Occupying one of the oldest homes on the famous art gallery–laden Canyon Road—thought to have been built in 1753, according to the original Spanish deed dated September 14, 1753—the Geronimo Restaurant is a favorite lunch and fine dining locale for tourists and locals alike. The first building owner, Geronimo Lopez, a former Spanish Army soldier, utilized the adobe structure as a family home and headquarters for his thirty-five-acre farm and orchard. While strolling down the uneven one-and-a-half mile-long sidewalks of the highly art-influenced Canyon Road, you would never guess this was once farmland that supported goats and sheep as well as fields of corn, alfalfa, and fruit.

The Geronimo has retained the old-world charm in architecture and nouveau cuisine. Expect a fine dining experience when you visit; this is a highly sought-after restaurant for those in the know. Locals once knew the Geronimo as the Rafael Borrego House, a family home; Borrego regularly

Valet parking at Geronimo is a necessity as it sits along an extremely narrow portion of the famous art-filled Canyon Road.

held galas and political meetings in the building. It was during this late 1800s timeframe that the distinctive long portal with hand-hewn tapered columns was installed.

For a time, the structure became endangered, and it was purchased by the Old Santa Fe Association to prevent further damage to the historical building. The association, in turn, resold it with strict covenants to ensure its continued preservation. In 1940, the house was selected by the Historic American Building Survey for study. Plans of the Geronimo exist in the Library of Congress's files for review.

In the 1960s, the Borrego House became the Three Cities of Spain restaurant and theater, which featured the coats of arms for Palencia, Valencia, and Mont Seurat around the dining room. Owners Bob Garrison and David Mein hosted a one-act play in the restaurant, which eventually spilled out into the streets to become a festival. By the 1970s, the structure had morphed once again into Ernie's, which featured Swiss cuisine. It would not become the Geronimo until 1990.

Serving seafood, smoked meats, elk, and bison as well as vegetarian selections with an excellent fine wine list, the Geronimo is graced with high ceilings, partially mirrored walls behind some of the bench seating; two large kiva-style fireplaces in the dining room with original wood floors; long, low windows; warm adobe walls; and white cloths on the tables. Since opening in 1990 under the ownership of Chris Harvey and Silin Cruz, Geronimo has been the recipient of several prestigious awards, including AAA's Four Diamond award for excellence and a spot on Open Table and Tripadvisor Travelers' Choice's Top 100 Restaurant list as well as the Forbes Travel Guide Four Star Award. Highly lauded for its attentive and trained staff, Geronimo prides itself on offering a "quiet luxury" dining experience for guests. Dress code is business casual, and the restaurant asks that no children under ten years of age visit "so as to not create dietary restrictions" on the creativity of the chef, since children tend not to have as palates as sophisticated as adults'.

One of the Geronimo signature cocktails is called Canyon Road Sunset, a heavenly creation with plum vodka, lavender plum bitters, Italian cherry syrup, citrus, and an edible flower, topped with a sparkling wine—quite a delightful experience for all your senses. Your dining experience at the Geronimo, on historic Canyon Road, will rival any establishment found on the West or East Coast, hands down.

Haunted Tales

As the land surrounding Canyon Road was once rich farming land, it makes sense that the ghost that reportedly haunts the Geronimo is that of a man dressed as a farmer. It's thought that the ghost is interested in the high-quality foods prepared there, as he has been seen by members of the restaurant staff in the kitchen watching the activities as well as looking pensively out of one of the restaurant's many windows. It is often wondered what Geronimo Lopez, should this be his ghost, thinks about what his humble abode has become.

THE PINK ADOBE
406 OLD SANTA FE TRAIL

Beginning its life as a military barracks when nearby pre–Civil War Fort Marcy was in its heyday, the Pink Adobe—or the Pink, as it is called by the

Across from the oldest church is the Pink Adobe Restaurant and Dragon Room bar. The former owner still holds court in the famous building.

locals—has been a restaurant of great fame, and visitors seek it out for an extraordinary authentic New Mexican meal with some Cajun influences. The typical Santa Fe–style adobe building is described as a "maze of intimate rooms" decorated with rustic furniture, brick floors, and vibrant pieces of artwork done by the original owner.

The Pink Adobe is built as a square with a courtyard in the center. The restaurant occupies one side and the Dragon Room the other. An unusual feature of the bar, called the Dragon Room, is a live tree growing out of the roof as the building was built around the tree. Many writers, artists, and celebrities have crossed the threshold of the Pink Adobe, and in its heyday, when owner Rosalea Murphy was alive, she wrote about the after-hours gatherings in the Dragon Room, where meetings of some of the most influential characters of that era were epic.

Haunted Tales

Although the Pink Adobe is not on most peoples' radar as a haunted place in Santa Fe, according to author Susan Blumenthal, she was able to garner a few stories from the regulars and the bartender during her visit. Blumenthal's hunch was that the Pink Adobe's proximity to the oldest church in the United States (across the street) and its history with the Pueblo Revolt of 1680 may possibly have led to at least a few residual presences still hanging around. She was right.

Susan was introduced to the story of Cajun expatriate Rosalea Murphy, the former owner of the Pink Adobe and an artist, who had a habit of sitting in a curved bank of seats in the corner of the Dragon Room with her dogs, Don Juan and Gina Lollobrigida, who were treated quite well—served water in highball glasses and fed large bowls of popcorn while people-watching with their owner. Rosalea's sense of humor came out as she told a reporter that most people thought she was sitting there all day "getting snockered," but her glass was always filled with only water. Rosalea was the originator of the Pink Adobe and its most recent apparition. Some have seen all of them sitting there still watching over her "baby" since her death in 2000 at age eighty-eight.

Rosalea was described as a character, the epitome of the spirit of Santa Fe. She was possibly also a poor driver, sometimes running over motorcycles in the restaurant parking lot with her black BMW and hitting the wall to the narrow entrance to the restaurant from time to time.

In Rosalea's defense, yes, she may not have been a great driver, but the roads and driveways in Santa Fe are extraordinarily narrow—first built as dirt paths for the burros who carried loads of piñon firewood to the various businesses from the mountains. Warning: These roads have not changed in many years since, which is why most residents drive small compact cars. It is highly recommended when visiting Santa Fe to utilize one of the public parking lots and explore this historic city on foot, just make sure to make this journey in good comfortable shoes. Buildings are often directly on the road, which makes it difficult, if not impossible, to expand the roadways at all.

Beloved by her staff, Rosalea Murphy, who was married four times and widowed once, never met a stranger, and according to a *Santa Fe New Mexican* article from July 8, 1994, written by John Villani, this powerhouse woman had a "devilish who-the-hell-cares laugh" and could be seen tooling around Santa Fe on her Harley Davidson motorcycle with a huge smile on her face. Rosalea sounds like a woman who truly loved life.

Rosalea was foremost an artist; this was her true calling and love. She was quoted as saying, "In 1944, I figured the restaurant could support me, and I could paint. But the restaurant became my monster; it kept growing. For the next fifteen years I only dabbled in painting. I prefer being an artist."

When the Pink Adobe was first opened with its thirty seats, Rosalea served her famous Dobe hamburgers and French onion soup for twenty-five cents and French apple pie slices for fifteen cents. A cup of coffee would cost you a whole nickel. She was also the cook, server, and dishwasher at this time. Although the prices are higher today, the same quality is there, and that's what brings celebrities, tourists, and locals back time and time again. Today, the Pink Adobe has six large dining rooms, each one featuring kiva fireplaces. A three-hundred-meal-night in the summer was not unheard of by 1988.

Another reported ghost in the Pink Adobe compound may stem from the discovery of a skull and potsherds when the foundation for the Dragon Room was being dug. Staff members have been able to identify this ghost as female, and they named her Mesera (which means "waitress"). Apparently, Mesera likes to fiddle with the pink trinkets that decorate some of the shelves. Items will be moved around constantly, and staff place the blame on Mesera, who is said to wear all brown. Mesera is also known to levitate tables, which startles the staff and new hires, as well as adding lemon wedges to drinks on occasion. New people are not told about the possibility of ghosts, to not scare them off but also to let them have their own experiences without prejudice.

Was Mesera a victim of the Pueblo Revolts? There is a good chance of this, since hundreds of people died in the violence that occurred, and this young lady may have been caught up in the chaos.

UPPER CRUST PIZZA
329 OLD SANTA FE TRAIL

Part of the Analco Barrio sector of Santa Fe, Upper Crust Pizza is situated west of the oldest house in the United States. The building it operates out of dates to the 1600s and is said to be part of the legendary Santa Fe "energy/spiritual vortex." This vortex has attracted energy healers and shamans from around the world to the City Different. There are only a few places on earth that are of the same caliber, including the Great Pyramids; Sedona, Arizona; and Machu Picchu—although scientists can show no true evidence of their existence.

Upper Crust Pizza has two locations and has been voted the best pizza in Santa Fe. This historic location downtown still has few invisible customers lurking in the shadows.

Nestled in a highly acclaimed neighborhood of Canyon Road—where art galleries, award-winning restaurants, boutiques, and historical destinations are everywhere—Upper Crust Pizza holds a prominent slot. As the narrow streets of Santa Fe can be a bit tricky to navigate, the free Santa Fe Pick-Up shuttle system is available for visitors and locals alike and runs every thirty minutes.

Using local favorite ingredients like piñon nuts and green chile, Upper Crust's pizza has been dubbed the Best Local Pizza by the *Santa Fe Reporter*. Add your favorite locally crafted or domestic beer or imported wine to your pie, and you have the makings of a wonderful afternoon or evening in the high desert. The restaurant offers gluten-free crust options as well as its traditional hand-tossed style. This is certainly not your chain restaurant–style pizza. Try their Grecian Gourmet, which brings a touch of Italy to Santa Fe with feta cheese, kalamata olives, bell peppers, mushrooms, and fresh garlic toppings. Or be brave and choose the New Mex, which features Tortilla Flats (another excellent Santa Fe restaurant on Cerrillos Road) red chile, shredded cheddar, onion, tomato, and chorizo—this would certainly be my first choice. Calzones, deli sandwiches, and salads are also available for your enjoyment. Top off this delicious meal with a piece of scrumptious cheesecake or a brownie.

Haunted Tales

Being a building of such advanced age (directly across the street from the oldest church in the United States) and having witnessed the tragedies of the Pueblo Revolt of 1680 right outside its doors, the Upper Crust Pizza building is said to be home to two ghosts. One is affectionately called Cowboy Jack, and the other is only known as the Lady.

As the years have gone by, activity in the pizzeria seems to have diminished, but the road directly outside the restaurant was part of the Santa Fe Trail, which brought visitors, soldiers, and frontiersmen from all parts of the burgeoning country to the New Mexico Territory. During the revolt, the Natives did not spare many of the Spanish settlers; the life of the Lady may have been tragically taken at that time. Outlaws and ruffians were plentiful in the territory, and Santa Fe was a hotbed of activity for cowboys to let off steam in the many saloons and brothels, such as that of Doña Gertrude Tulles in the heart of the growing, raucous City Different.

Situated in the historic Barrio de Analco district, Upper Crust Pizza has an enviable spot in close quarters with many historical sites.

The Guadalupe Café nearby has closed—unfortunately, as it had many great ghost tales to tell itself. Maybe the bread- and bowl-throwing ghost in the red dress will move on down the street to the Pink Adobe or Upper Crust Pizza if she gets bored all alone—or perhaps she likes the solitude of the closed building. Peek in the window; you never know what you might see!

El Farol
808 Canyon Road

Another restaurant not on everyone's haunted radar is El Farol (the Lantern) in Santa Fe. It was once widely known that if the lantern was lit, the restaurant was open. It is said to have been built in 1835 by the Vigil family and was known then as La Cantina Del Cañon (the Bar of Canyon Road), which makes El Farol the oldest restaurant and bar in New Mexico. The restaurant is heralded as "Santa Fe's most historic and iconic bar and restaurant" on its website, and it's proud to share a review of the bar by the *New York Times* as the reviewer called it "one of the best bars on earth"—high praise indeed.

As a hot night spot on Canyon Road, El Farol is on the Santa Fe Margarita Trail, which features more than fifty locations to visit with your margarita passport.

Signature cocktails and margaritas top the list as guest favorites, paired with an amazing assortment of tapas. As the restaurant is part of the famed Santa Fe Margarita Trail, you can get your passport stamped to earn prizes. (Visit https://www.santafe.org for more details.) Are you brave enough to try the prickly pear or spicy jalapeño margaritas?

Laughter, dance, and music accompanied by colorful murals painted by renowned artist Alfred Morang make a visit to El Farol a complete event. The weekends feature a live flamenco dinner show. Be warned: This intensely powerful experience, which includes a three-course meal and a lively flamenco dance show presented by talented and classically trained members of the National Institute of Flamenco, will run several hundred dollars per couple, but all the reviews state this unforgettable experience is well worth the expense for a possibly once-in-a-lifetime memory. Live music events are also available and vary depending on the time of year. Reservations are highly recommended.

Haunting Tales

Despite the amount of life that El Farol presents to the world, it is said its ghosts are on the mild side. Possibly they cannot compete with their surroundings, although Santa Fe was once the epitome of a Wild West town, complete with soldiers, travelers on the Santa Fe Trail, cowboys, trappers, outlaws, shady ladies, and gamblers. The sunken La Cantina Del Cañon had famous patrons such as author Willa Cather, socialite Mabel Dodge Luhan, and even actor John Wayne. Bullet holes, harking back to the rougher days of the cantina, can still be seen—said to have resulted from someone taking a shot at the bartender. Horses are known to have been ridden into the cantina on a regular basis as well.

The presence of mural artist Alfred Morang can be felt since he loved to hang out at El Farol during his lifetime. The cantina often toasts the amazing artist, known to many as Santa Fe's version of Toulouse-Lautrec. The restaurant/cantina is proud of its family atmosphere and claims that this factor was one of Morang's biggest reasons for enjoying the building and its staff; the other was that the murals were done to settle the artist's tab between the years of 1948 and 1952. Tragedy occurred on Easter morning in 1997 when a fire broke out in El Farol, but somehow, the murals survived the ravages of the flames with barely a burn mark. Many believe this was significant to Morang's spirit, since it was a studio fire that ended the artist's life in 1958—they believe his work was protected by his ghost. The cantina features a cocktail called Alfred's Special, in homage to Morang's home state of Maine. Rye whiskey, Heering Cherry Liqueur, and a splash of absinthe form a cocktail that the creator suggests was inspired by one of Morang's early landscapes.

Staff say there is an *embrujo* (enchantment) within the adobe walls that demands to be respected as almost a living entity. The walls breathe and move with the earth. These walls have been lovingly maintained over the

With alcohol comes trouble. This front door was the site of a tragic double murder. Through fire and tragedy, El Farol has survived.

years by many sets of hands and have seen much violence. One of the former owners was fatally stabbed by the front door; when his wife tried to help, she was also stabbed.

One of the ghostly activities most reported by the staff is the strange noises heard on El Farol's cantina roof. Strangely enough, many night staff refuse to stay late or alone to close. Owner David Salazar has said he thinks the sounds on the roof may be made by the ghost known as the Lady in Red, a former waitress. This is also the name of a mural painted by Morang of the vibrant woman, who had a drinking problem and often got up on stage to dance wildly before ending her shift.

If these are indeed the fun-loving spirits who refuse to leave the festive environment of El Farol, you will be in good company as you sip on your margaritas and eat the delectable dishes offered.

TAOS

Taos is often touted as New Mexico's most haunted city and judging by the amount of violence that has occurred there, and the strange feelings experienced during the author's visits, this is a true assessment. Taos is also home to the Taos Pueblo, which has been continuously occupied for over one thousand years. With a population hovering around six thousand, Taos is a small village with a lot of culture and experiences to offer. This stunning city within a city is a masterpiece of architecture and ingenuity. Home to world-class skiing, Taos is a resort destination for thousands hoping to tackle the challenging slopes.

Taos began its history as Don Fernandez de Taos in the late 1700s, and since at least AD 900 it has been home to the Tewa-speaking people, who lived relatively peacefully until the area was discovered by the Spanish conquistadors in 1540 during the Coronado expedition. The relationship between the Taos Pueblo inhabitants and the Spaniards was rocky, and the Taos Pueblo played a large role in the Pueblo Revolt of 1680, which succeed in driving most, if not all, of the Spaniards who survived the revolt out of the region to the El Paso, Texas area. Little by little, the Spaniards began to trickle back into the Taos area to start establishing settlements once again but not until the late 1700s.

As a magnet for artists, Taos has been home to greats such as Georgia O'Keeffe; members of the Taos Artist Colony, including Joseph Henry

Sharp; and contemporary Native artist R.C. Gorman. Mabel Dodge Luhan was a huge influence and patron of the arts who supported and promoted the varied styles of works coming from the tiny village. Other artists who flocked to Taos encompassed well-known photographers Edward S. Curtis and Ansel Adams as well as many writers of the era, such as D.H. Lawrence of *Lady Chatterley's Lover* fame (whose secret collection of erotic art is displayed behind a curtain at the Hotel La Fonda de Taos). The tradition continues as artists of every medium are drawn to the beauty of the Taos landscape and open spaces.

It is not uncommon to spot a famous actor or actress walking casually along the narrow streets of Taos or in one of the historic bars. When you visit, keep a keen eye for celebrities as you do some people-watching while soaking up the high desert atmosphere. The sidewalks are narrow and uneven, so do pay some attention to where you are stepping as you look.

Taos bore witness to an enormous amount of tragedy in its past, which included many massacres and uprisings. If the adobe buildings lining the streets (which used to be burro paths and are still very narrow), could tell their stories, they would be harrowing tales. Bent Street—named for the first territorial governor of the state, Charles Bent, whose home was located

Beautifully situated on the Taos Plaza, Hotel La Fonda De Taos is sometimes mistaken for its Santa Fe cousin due to their similar names.

about one block north of Taos Plaza—was the site of two of the most brutal massacres in New Mexico history, the first being the Pueblo Revolt of 1680, in which over four hundred Spaniards and Spanish sympathizers were slaughtered and the rest pushed south as far as possible.

During the Taos Pueblo Revolt on January 19, 1847, Governor Bent and his family were living in a home on the street that bears his name. Unable to keep their attackers at bay, the women and children of the Bent household dug holes in the adobe walls of the home to escape before being overrun and killed. Charles Bent was not as lucky: When the rioters broke down the door, Bent was shot with arrows and scalped in front of his family before their escape. Several other American officials, Hispanic sympathizers, were scalped and killed during this attack as well.

After killing many more in Taos, the enraged group moved to the nearby communities of Mora, Arroyo Hondo, Red River Canyon, Cienega Creek, and Las Vegas, where the carnage continued until July 9, 1847. The Moreno Valley area is also the site of much paranormal activity. On the American side, over 367 people were killed and 103 wounded. On the attackers' side, only 11 were killed (although some accounts state it was closer to 150), but over 400 were captured by the United States Army during the initial attack. Those captured men were brought to trial after the bloodshed ceased, and many of the insurgents were hanged for their actions.

The reason behind the revolt was a demand from the Pueblo people for the release of some of their people from the American jail. The Pueblo people felt they had been poorly treated by the United States soldiers and that their people were falsely imprisoned. When this demand was denied, the revolt resulted. All Americans or their collaborators were targeted.

Events such as this revolt set back efforts for New Mexico to become a state for another sixty-five years. New Mexico was seen as too violent, and its people having been under Spanish and Mexican rule for so long, their loyalty was deeply questioned by Washington, D.C. Fortunately, New Mexico was finally allowed to join the Union and gained statehood on January 6, 1912. Unfortunately, even today, New Mexico is forgotten as a state, but we are working on changing that fact.

Built in the 1880s, an elaborate tunnel system was established under the town of Taos—mainly for safety reasons, due to the constant Comanche raids of that time. These tunnels were (and still are) accessible from most of the shops that line Doña Luz on Guadalupe Plaza.

The distinct possibility of the presence of otherworldly beings roaming the historic streets of Taos cannot be discounted—as Taos is also considered

Three witches are said to be buried under these concrete blocks; their names have been erased from history.

to have a vortex that can project both positive and negative energy. This vortex is thought to be the source for the "Taos hum," which only sensitive people seem to hear. On top of all these reasons, it is thought that there are three Taos witches who are allegedly buried in the Kit Carson Memorial Cemetery, lending to the overall mystique of Taos. They are covered in asphalt to prevent them from rising out of their graves; the only items marking the graves are crumbled pieces of concrete and rebar. It is said that their headstones were blown up to forever mask their identities. So, if you're searching for a good Halloween destination, haunted Taos is certainly highly recommended.

Byzantium Restaurant/La Loma Bar
112 Cam de la Placita, Suite B

Although the Byzantium Restaurant was temporarily closed, it has once again reopened, so this author deems the story of one of the violent incidents that occurred around the building worth telling—as this reported spirit sighting was important to the ambiance of the Taos paranormal experience. The Byzantium Restaurant has labeled itself an "intimate, upscale establishment featuring New American plates and wine in a low-lit, moody atmosphere." This description is true since you'll find there are only seven tables for service in the small room with darkly painted walls when you walk through the arched doorway of what appears to be a private home.

Haunted Tales

Once a raucous basement watering hole in Taos, La Loma Bar was the site of many bar fights and quarrels, including one that involved a man who stabbed his girlfriend as the result of a heated argument. The woman stumbled out into the street toward Ledoux Street. It is said she left a trail of bloody handprints on the walls and doors on her way as she cried pitifully in pain. This woman was dubbed La Llorona of Ledoux, and she is said to make an appearance on the Day of the Dead (Dia De Los Muertos). La Llorona is a famous tale in New Mexico and "Old Mexico" that involves the legend of a woman who was trying to win the favor of a man (some say he was her cheating husband) and thought her two children were hindering her chances for happiness. As a result, the woman drowned the children in an acequia (ditch). After her drastic actions, the man still spurned her. She is now condemned to walk the acequias everywhere in search of her children. La Llorona is called the Weeping Woman since her anguished cries can be heard. Children are warned not to go near the ditches or else "La Llorona will get them." Is this a clever scare tactic to keep the kids in line? Maybe, but it seems to work very well.

HISTORIC TAOS INN/DOC MARTIN'S RESTAURANT/ ADOBE BAR 125 PASEO DEL PUEBLO

Along the narrow main street of Taos is an inn and bar that has seen more history than even the historians may know. The striking pueblo-style adobe walls of the inn reach up from the street, which originally was a burro trail

Historic Taos Inn is the heart of the Taos downtown historic district and is the place to see or be seen by visiting celebrities.

when the inn was first built. Within a few minutes' walk of most of the historic attractions Taos has to offer, the Historic Taos Inn, which was built in the early 1800s, is a haven for celebrities and locals alike; it is the place people go to see and be seen in Taos.

Inside the lobby of the inn is a large wooden structure that was once used as the community well. Dr. Thomas Paul Martin, known by the locals as Doc, purchased what was then the largest adobe home in town, which is part of the hotel complex in Taos. As Doc was Taos County's first physician, you can imagine how busy he was with his practice, which was housed in the current Doc Martin's Restaurant. As the only physician, Doc made house calls while traveling in his horse and buggy. Many Taoseños were born in the restaurant, which was a private alcove in the doctor's day.

Doc's wife, Helen, played a large part of the burgeoning Taos art scene as a talented batik artist and the sister-in-law of Bert Phillips, who was one of the founders of the Taos Society of Artists. It was not unusual for Doc to find a houseful of prominent artists in his home at any given time. Sadly, Doc passed away in 1935, and the only hotel in Taos also burned to the ground that year. Helen took this opportunity to purchase more of the buildings surrounding the original complex and opened the Hotel Martin in 1936. This complex was placed on the National and State Registers of Historic

One of the most striking features of the Historic Taos Inn's lobby is the well, which once provided water for the entire community.

There is no better place than the Taos Inn's bar to listen to some live music while enjoying their famous Cowboy Buddha Margaritas.

Places in 1982, and the name was changed to the Historic Taos Inn. It is now a historic landmark.

There is an ornate well with a stained-glass cupola inside the lobby of the Historic Taos Inn, which was the community well when the lobby was an open-air plaza and is today a prime locale for great conversations and libations.

The Adobe Bar is known as the living room of Taos as it features live music every night and its world-famous Cowboy Buddha Margaritas. "This is still a place where everybody knows everybody," according to author Ashley M. Biggers for *New Mexico Magazine* in her 2022 article about the Historic Taos Inn and Adobe Bar. Who knows, there may be a few of the original Taoseños joining in on the fun as well.

Haunted Tales

Inconspicuously nestled behind the Taos Inn kitchen is the site of a horrific crime scene where the most hated man in Taos was killed.

The Historic Taos Inn is the murder site of Arthur Manby, a wealthy but much-hated man who took great pleasure in crooked land-grabbing. He was found murdered and missing his head (the head is supposed to be still missing). It was reported Manby's poor German shepherd dogs were locked up with the corpse and ate the head, something the traumatized animal paid for with his life even without evidence of the truth. The gruesome scene is on the restaurant premises, but it is only part of the hotel's history. According to staff, the public can request to stay in this room if they are brave enough.

Night staff report seeing salt and pepper shakers and napkins being shoved horizontally along a shelf in the kitchen as if a hand was sweeping them off, causing some of them to break on the floor without reason. Disembodied voices were heard coming from a room connected to the kitchen when no one was checked into the room, shaking the night audit staff—especially when they heard their names spoken and no one was in the building.

The most haunted rooms of the hotel are located behind the kitchen in the courtyard. It is said that the bodies of people who died in winter were stored in these rooms since the ground was too frozen to bury them. Footfalls and jingling spurs can sometimes be heard on the second floor of the hotel outside a room where several dark shadows have been observed.

Glassware moving on its own and the lights turning on by themselves in the Adobe Bar make for a fun time for the bartenders, who take the activity with a grain of salt.

ALLEY CANTINA
121 TERESINA LANE

The building in which the Alley Cantina is housed is part of the original Taos Plaza, and it is said to be over four hundred years old. Pueblo Indians were responsible for building several of the walls of what is now Alley Cantina when it served as an outpost along the Chihuahua Trail.

The building was the site of Territorial Governor Charles Bent's office, and its thick adobe walls have seen much tragedy during their four centuries of existence as it was within them that the Bent massacre occurred during the Taos Pueblo Revolt of 1847. It was here that Bent's young daughter Teresina—for whom the street is named—witnessed the brutal murder and scalping of her father before being released by the Natives.

This tragic building became El Patio Restaurant in 1944 and remained so until it was purchased in 1996 by Buzz Waterhouse, who, after some renovations, reopened the restaurant as the Alley Cantina. Stepping into the Alley Cantina is like stepping into history. The kiva fireplaces, latillas, viga ceilings, polished cement floors, and white stucco walls scream New Mexico style. The cantina itself is covered by skylights, giving warmth and protection from the elements.

Dishes recommended from the menu by many reviewers include the chicken enchiladas and the adovada, a red chile pork stew. Don't forget the famous margaritas, which complement the New Mexican cuisine perfectly.

Then-owner Buzz Waterhouse brought in live musical acts and his restaurant was the place to go after everything else shut down as it stayed open into the early morning. Waterhouse was partial to blues music and featured it regularly. Two of the artists highlighted were local vocalists Cullin Winter and Christine Autumn (Robinson). Open mic is still a tradition at the Alley Cantina.

Haunted Tales

Allegedly Taos's oldest bar, the Alley Cantina is smack dab in the middle of the paranormal vortex in Taos. As mentioned earlier, Governor Bent's daughter Teresina witnessed her father's death, which must have traumatized her for the rest of her life. Bent's family never returned home after the revolt, so the young girl must not have got closure or remained in disbelief about the horrors she saw as a child. Teresina is said to still roam the halls and rooms of the Alley Cantina, possibly still searching for her father. Servers and patrons alike have seen items moving on their own as well as candles lighting by themselves. Could this be Teresina?

Former owner Buzz Waterhouse was asked if El Patio (Alley Cantina) was haunted when he owned it, to which he is said to have replied, "If you don't believe there are ghosts in this building, I invite you to spend some time here alone around two thirty in the morning; strange things happen." Waterhouse was a former food and beverage manager at the Historic Taos Inn at one time and probably ran into a few of their spirits as well, so he was well-versed in the paranormal.

Some of the incidents reported by staff and patrons alike include candles lighting and items moving on their own in the dining room. Patrons have reported the creepy feeling of someone wrapping their arms around them in a ghostly embrace in the ladies' restroom.

CIMARRON

The village of Cimarron, first officially chartered in 1859, is situated on the gorgeous eastern slopes of the Sangre De Cristo (Blood of Christ) Mountains. Living up to the meaning of its name, "wild" or "unbroken" Cimarron was one of the wildest villages in the New Mexico Territory but eventually became the Colfax County seat by 1872—only to be replaced by Springer, New Mexico, in 1881.

Beginning its life as a stage stop for the Mountain Branch of the Santa Fe Trail and a major hub for the many cattle trails and mining communities, like nearby Elizabethtown, that surround it, Cimarron attracted some colorful characters in its heyday. As part of the enormous Maxwell Land Grant, estimated at 1.7 million acres, Cimarron had over 7,500 square feet of corrals to hold the herds as they waited to be taken to Oklahoma and Kansas. The eastern slopes of the mountains provided a great source of vast grasslands.

The involvement and interference of the corrupt Santa Fe Ring in territorial politics led to the killing of a Methodist circuit preacher by the name of Reverend Franklin J. Tolby, who had made it known through his sermons and letters that he was not a fan of this dangerous group. People who challenged the Santa Fe Ring generally did not have a long life. As it was,

This granite headstone was erected after the death of Reverend Franklin J. Tolby, the catalyst that ignited the bloody Colfax County War.

Tolby was a close friend of gunfighter and cattleman Clay Allison, who took it upon himself to avenge the killing of the preacher, whose murder is still unsolved and has led to numerous deaths in and around Cimarron—especially in the Lambert Inn (now the St. James Hotel). Allison was once courted by the Santa Fe Ring to do its dirty work of removing homesteaders from the land grant, but he saw the light and was able to break free. Allison was greatly feared in the region—even by the ring. These events contributed to the start of the Colfax County War.

After twelve long years and over two hundred casualties, the Colfax County War came to a halt, but Cimarron would long wear the scars of this conflict. Today, Cimarron is home to the Philmont Scout Ranch, which brings in thousands of scouts each year to participate in the annual jamboree. As a side note, the ranch is also haunted. Scouts have reported seeing a man dressed like a cowboy (thought to be Tom "Black Jack" Ketchum) and lost scouts on the many forested trails. Within the ranch property is said to be the most haunted place in New Mexico: Urraca Mesa. This mesa is sacred to the Ute and Jicarilla Apache people, and there are many reports of protective cat totems around the foot of the mesa, placed there to protect their sacred grounds.

Camping, mountain biking, hunting, hiking, and fly fishing easily doubles the town's population of 792 in the spring and summer months. As a gateway to the Enchanted Circle Scenic Byway, Cimarron Canyon provides a feast for the eyes when the cottonwoods, aspens, and oak trees change colors starting in late September along the Cimarron River, which flows close to the side of the road. The majestic Palisade Sill is an example of a porphyritic dacite sill, which formed over forty million years ago and resulted in the three-hundred-foot cliffs at an elevation of eight thousand feet that line the highway between Cimarron and Eagle Nest. This is a wonderfully picturesque drive—be ready to make numerous stops to take many photos.

St. James Hotel 617 Collison Avenue

Built in 1872, the St. James Hotel has been a staple of the town of Cimarron ever since and is the town's largest employer. A hub of entertainment and commerce, the St. James started life as the Lambert Saloon, named for its builder, Henri Lambert, who at one time was a personal chef for both Presidents Lincoln and Grant during the American Civil War era. It was Lambert's dream to move west and open his own hotel.

Lambert's dream came true in 1872 when the inn and saloon was completed, and his establishment soon became the hub of the region. The town of Cimarron was the center of the cattle industry as it was along several well-traveled cattle trails, most notably the Goodnight-Loving Trail. This meant cowboys fresh off the trail made a beeline to the Lambert Inn for some drinks and entertainment. This generally meant trouble followed them as well.

One of the Lambert Inn's most colorful patrons was Robert "Clay" Allison, a cattleman, gunfighter, and all-around bad man. Allison was said to have been the most watched gunfighter ever since no one knew when his mind or attitude would change on a dime, especially when he was drinking—which he did constantly. Allison is thought to have placed most of the four hundred bullet holes found in the tin ceiling of the bar, which were found during remodeling. When Allison was "in his cups," he tended to dance on the bar naked. One thing about Cimarron: It was not boring.

Other visitors to the inn were notables such as Kit Carson, Annie Oakley, Will James, William "Buffalo Bill" Cody, Jesse James, Governor Lew Wallace, and Tom "Black Jack" Ketchum, to name a few. Many of these people have rooms named for them in the original portion of the hotel.

Much like in Taos, there are rumors of tunnels under the narrow streets in town, which allowed the fine upstanding gentlemen of the town to visit the many brothels that lined the streets or provided a means of escape for outlaws when they were on the run.

Haunted Tales

One of the St. James's leading ghost tales involves a gambler named Thomas J. Wright, who spent a great deal of time in the St. James Saloon at the poker

Described as the most haunted hotel in New Mexico, the St. James Hotel has seen much tragedy and has at least twenty-six deaths to its credit.

St. James Saloon was a hot spot for local outlaws Clay Allison and Davy Crockett, who placed four hundred bullet holes in the ceiling.

table. Usually not considered a highly skilled card player, T.J. (as he was known around Cimarron) would not let a little bad luck stand in the way as he knew one day it would change for him—and he was right.

One particularly uncharacteristic lucky night of gambling resulted in Wright winning the St. James from its owner, Henri Lambert. What happened next is not known, other than the fact that Lambert was most likely not happy with these events. Possibly with some boastful comments, Wright decided to retire for the night and relish his sudden windfall. The gambler made it to the door of his room (Room 18), where he was shot in the back—reportedly by Henri Lambert, but this was never proven. The gunshot caused T.J. to lurch forward into his room, where he died.

The St. James used to rent out T.J.'s room for the night, but so many people left in the middle of the night—or they heard later that something tragic had happened to the guests—that the proprietors decided to lock up the room. Privacy seems to suit T.J., who stays in his room for the most part. Although I was graciously let into T.J.'s room to take photographs for my books, I was not told until later about the tragic happenings that befell people who were allowed in the room, but thankfully, T.J. took mercy on me, and I was fine.

During my stay, I booked the Mary Lambert room (named for Henri Lambert's second wife; his first wife was also, ironically, named Mary), which was the closest to T.J.'s, as it was catty-corner to the haunted room and was also reportedly haunted. My goal was to test both reports of the rooms being haunted. It's said that Mary Lambert likes to tickle the toes of male guests, and the aroma of her rose perfume can be detected as well. (Nothing was experienced in this room during the author's stay.)

The rooms on the second floor are accessible only by utilizing a narrow-carpeted staircase. They feature beautifully painted transom windows over the original wooden doors and are decorated as close to the original décor as possible. Wooden door and window frames as well as original wood floors add to the ambiance.

After listening to a folk singer in the saloon, I decided to retire for the evening, but before leaving the bar, I bought a jigger of whiskey for T.J. as a thank-you for letting me invade his space. As I placed the jigger on the transom ledge, I tapped lightly on the door to say thank-you and good night and went across the hall to my room. Another couple had the same idea and placed theirs shortly after. During the night, the heavy scent of cigar smoke crept under the wooden door and permeated my room, and I heard the sound of footsteps in the hallway. Knowing no smoking was allowed in the

Resident ghost Thomas J. Wright occupies Room 18, where the gambler died after being shot in the back after winning the hotel in a poker game.

hotel, I found it odd but, quite frankly, thought it was possibly the hotel staff. The next morning, as I was leaving, I noticed that the jigger of whiskey I'd placed on the window was empty, while the other was still full.

Does this prove it was T.J.? No. Could it have been a member of the hotel staff, even though I was told they lock up and leave for the night? Yes. But I like to think the unlucky gambler was there and appreciated his midnight whiskey.

CLAYTON

Clayton is a railroad town, which is evidenced by one train that may come through town at two o'clock in the morning during your stay. If you are not prepared for this, it may make for a startling situation. The town is located at the end of a desolate two-lane highway that was at one time the Cimarron Cutoff, also known as the Cimarron Route of the Santa Fe Trail, and was part of the Comancheria (Comanche Land) in the mid-1800s. The area is landmarked by the Rabbit Ears Mountain and the Capulin Volcano, which are both now national monuments. In prehistoric times, Clayton was heavily used by the dinosaurs of the region. Evidence of their presence can be found at the Clayton Lake State Park and Dinosaur Trackways, said to be the most extensive examples of dinosaur tracks in North America.

Located only ten miles from the Texas border and eleven miles from the Oklahoma border, the town receives visitors from both states as Clayton is home to several attractions. The Clayton Lake State Park and the Capulin Volcano National Monument are both definite stops to put on your bucket list. At Capulin Volcano, only three miles away, it turns red in the summer, not from lava but from millions of lady beetles, commonly known as ladybugs, who are blown there with the wind every year to hibernate before continuing with their migrations each February. They're a sight to behold—not to mention the ability to see five states from the top of the volcano's rim.

The town has a population of just under three thousand people today, and the land surrounding the small town has been settled by Native Americans for at least ten thousand years. The town was a stop on the Cimarron Cutoff of the Santa Fe Trail, which was said to shorten the trail by one hundred miles, bringing commerce to the Clayton region since 1821. Huge cattle trails such as the famed Goodnight-Loving Trail passed through the area as well, as cattle were driven to the stockyards of Fort Worth, Texas.

Rancher Stephen Dorsey gained rights to the land through which the railroad would eventually run in 1887, and his ranch manager, John C. Hill, surveyed the townsite, which was named after Clayton C. Dorsey, the son of Stephen W. Dorsey, a senator from Arkansas who had established the Triangle Dot Ranch, which spanned both Union and Colfax Counties.

The village of Clayton played host to President Theodore Roosevelt on April 14, 1905, during his trip via railroad through the country. Everything was looking up for the town until it was hit with what locals called the black roller on May 28, 1937, which was a monster dust cloud (today we call them haboobs) that measured 1,500 feet high and at least one mile across. This cloud did considerable damage to the town and ushered in the dust bowl to this region. Thanks to the Works Progress Administration (WPA), the community was rebuilt, and it is now once again a prosperous town on the windswept eastern plains of New Mexico.

HOTEL EKLUND
15 MAIN STREET

Nestled conveniently next to the railroad tracks that bisect the town of Clayton, New Mexico, the Hotel Eklund has stood proud since 1892, a survivor of a bygone era. Built from honed limestone bricks, the stately two-story hotel is a historic icon on Clayton. Purchased by Carl Eklund in 1894,

"Wine, dine, and recline" is the motto of the iconic 1892 three-story stone Hotel Eklund in the historic downtown district of Clayton, New Mexico.

the property expanded into what is available today: twenty-four guest rooms, two dining rooms, and a saloon.

The Hotel Eklund is a charming blast from the past. Its saloon, built in 1892, is touted as "one of New Mexico's most iconic bars" by the Eklund's website, and you would swear Tom "Black Jack" Ketchum himself could walk into it at any time—even though he didn't drink, but he did like to dance. The saloon features a front and back bar that once supported pool, carom, monte, poker, and craps tables. Live music can be found on the weekends, which will have your toes tapping in the Wild West setting.

Victorian furnishings in the dining room of the Hotel Eklund lend an elegant setting to the Old West feel of the hotel. Personally, I would recommend the enchilada plate if you wanted a great taste of New Mexican cuisine. Since Clayton is a ranching community, the locally sourced steaks are said to be some of the best in the state.

Haunted Tales

Clayton boasts of being one of the most haunted towns in New Mexico, due mostly to its violent history. The Hotel Eklund has a couple of ghost stories to investigate, one being that of Irene, a maid who is said to walk the halls of the third floor and stay in Room 307 since it is her favorite. One often-told story concerns a female guest who took to her bed with a migraine and, in the morning, thanked her husband for being so attentive to her by massaging her head during the night. This show of gratefulness surprised her husband, as he did not stay awake at all during her episode. Many think it was Irene.

One of the Hotel Eklund's most famous spirits is that of Thomas (Tom) "Black Jack" Ketchum. A train robber and cattle thief, Ketchum also had the distinction of being the only train robber in New Mexico to have been hanged for this crime. Black Jack had been through quite a bit before his hanging. He attempted a train robbery by himself, resulting in an amputated arm, which caused him so much distress after his arrest that he attempted to swallow the pins that held his bandage together. But this was just the beginning.

Since Black Jack was ruggedly handsome, with a prominent black mustache and chiseled jaw, the ladies of the town took it upon themselves to feed the prisoner homemade meals. As a result, Tom gained about twenty

Shunned even in death: The lonely grave of executed train robber Thomas "Black Jack" Ketchum is in the center of the Clayton Cemetery.

pounds during his incarceration, which led to something catastrophic in the future. Due to a sequence of errors—the rope being too short or too long, depending on which story you believe; the extra weight going unaccounted for; and the fact that no one in the county had ever performed a hanging before; what happened to Tom "Black Jack" Ketchum during his hanging was horrific. When the trapdoor was sprung, the convict was jerked down so hard that he literally lost his head. Horrible images exist of the botched execution that would make your skin crawl. The undertaker sewed Ketchum's head back onto his shoulders while it was still clad in the black hood that he was wearing at the gallows.

After his death, Black Jack was buried in Clayton Boot Hill, which was located in the open prairie in 1901, but his remains were disinterred and moved to the Clayton Cemetery by 1933. Interestingly the cemetery was divided between Catholics and Protestants, and neither side wanted the outlaw in their midst, so Ketchum was buried under a tree in the middle of them both.

Black Jack's ghost is said to still be wandering the hallways of the Union County Courthouse, in front of which he was executed. He likes to make appearances at the Hotel Eklund from time to time since it's said he loved their chicken dinners.

EAGLE NEST

LAGUNA VISTA LODGE, HISTORIC RESTAURANT AND SALOON 51 E. THERMA STREET

In the beautiful resort town of Eagle Nest, originally known as Therma, is a historical hotel that has a haunted past, which includes the restaurant. Serving as the gateway to the famed Enchanted Circle Scenic Byway, Eagle Nest began life as a gold-mining community. At an elevation of approximately 8,200 feet, the mountain oasis features the stunningly beautiful Eagle Nest Lake, which provides world-class fishing, including ice fishing in the winter, weather permitting.

The village of Eagle Nest is situated between the historic town of Cimarron and the resort town of Angel Fire. Mountain biking, hiking, and

One of the most beautiful drives in New Mexico is at the gateway to the Enchanted Circle and follows the Cimarron River and Palisades Sill.

leaf-peeping in the fall months is one of the tiny town's biggest draws today. In the early days of the region, land disputes led to multiple murders, a large outlaw presence, and the formation of vigilante groups. Gold mining in the nearby town of Elizabethtown had played out by the early 1900s, leaving the once-prosperous town destitute. By 1918, the Eagle Nest Dam had been constructed, and a massive lake was formed from the waters of the Cimarron River. This provided much-needed water for mining, farming, and ranching operations.

Eagle Nest remained a peaceful community until the 1920s, during Prohibition, when illegal gambling, drinking, and dancing became the thing to do in the village. By 1940, a booming business of slot machines was prevalent, but things soon changed when the authorities began raiding the saloons and dance halls with axes in hand. It is rumored that once the machines were hacked up by axes, then were thrown into the Eagle Nest Lake. This rumor is substantiated by claims of slot machines being spotted in the lake whenever the water level is low.

Today, Eagle Nest is a haven for fisherman, hikers, bikers, campers, ATV activities, and the like as it is now a New Mexico State Park. Also, if you travel approximately fifteen miles toward the historic town of Cimarron, you will be able to follow along the Cimarron River through the Cimarron Palisades. Here, you can partake in fly fishing, hiking, and camping while drinking in the sheer beauty that surrounds you.

Haunted Tales

The swinging doors of the Laguna Vista Lodge, Historic Restaurant and Saloon are reminiscent of the Wild West days from which the village sprang. Stepping into the front foyer of the restaurant, you are greeted with original furniture and decorative items from the building's heyday, when it was known as the Guney or El Monte (depending on which version of history you read) after being established in 1898. In need of building materials to complete the lodge, the owner reportedly used stolen railroad ties. Some of these ties are still visible today in one of the staff-only storage rooms. The ties were originally slated for use to build a new hotel in nearby Ute Park, but when the hotel owner returned to the area after transporting the ties for two summers, he found they'd been stolen—and lo and behold, a new hotel had been built in Therma.

Top: Harking back to the Old West days, the Laguna Vista Lodge, Historic Restaurant and Saloon has secrets to tell but won't give them up easily.

Bottom: This dress, thought to be the wedding dress of the widowed bride Eleanor, is a stark reminder of how life can change in a heartbeat.

One of the busiest saloons in the region, El Monte, had a seventeen-foot hand-dug well and several ice houses behind the structure and has had several owners as well as name changes during its existence.

Some of the ghostly occurrences reported by the staff and a psychic are perpetrated by twenty-two spirits who refuse to leave the mountain property. One employee was working in the kitchen by herself when she heard a vacuum cleaner turn on in the dining room. When the staff member went to investigate, the vacuum was tucked in the corner silent and unplugged.

A former manager stated he heard the piano being played by an unseen entity after watching a dining room chair being pulled up to the front of the instrument. Today a sign graces the piano stating, "I am older than you, do not touch."

In the early days, the top floor of the lodge was a hotel as well as a brothel, which housed several ladies of the night. One sad story is connected to these rooms above the restaurant. A young newly married couple spent the night in the hotel. The next morning, the husband left to go on a hunting expedition but never returned. The bride, named Eleanor, was unable to pay the bill and was left destitute, so she resorted to becoming a resident of the brothel as a saloon girl. Owners are not certain if Eleanor worked in one of the upstairs rooms, but some historians state she became the madam at some point. Many visitors have reported a woman in a white gown searching the hotel for her husband. Eleanor is also known to call certain staff members by their names. It is thought Eleanor died of a broken heart but will not leave the hotel just in case her husband returns.

Past managers swear another saloon girl haunts the restaurant and is quite choosy about the type of music that is played in the establishment, even after hours. Staff members state that if any music other than country or classic rock is played, the barmaid spirit changes the channel on the radio—especially if rap is playing. At times, the ghost makes her preferences well known and becomes violent if they are not followed. Marble rolling pins, pots, pans, and kitchen utensils are her weapons of choice, flying across the room without any visible means of support. The spirit also chooses how long the music plays and turns the radio back on when it's turned off, even when it's unplugged and without batteries.

There are also reports of a young boy who is mostly heard in one of the upstairs rooms. The boy has been heard crying loudly and playing in the hallway off the secret staircase used by respectable townsmen and traveling politicians on their way to the horse races in Raton, New Mexico. Orbs have been observed, especially during live music shows.

One of the most relayed stories that comes from the lodge involves the two-year-old daughter of the manager, who had jingle bells placed on her shoes so they would always know where the young girl was in the building. One day, the manager saw her young daughter enter the kitchen with a stricken look on her face. When asked what was wrong, the girl stated, "The lady told me to stop making noise." The manager was upset that someone would speak to her daughter this way and asked her to show her the lady. The girl led her mother into the dining room, pointed, and stated, "That lady"—but there was no one visible to the manager in the room. Although the manager did not see anyone, her daughter insisted on having the bells removed.

The brothel was in operation until 1971; a woman by the name of Toots was the madam at that time. Toots, who had been working with her daughters, aged fourteen and fifteen, in the brothel, caught wind of an impending raid by authorities. The woman and her daughters left before the raid and have not been seen again in Eagle Nest; thus, the brothel closed.

Eagle Nest Café
25 E. Therma Street NM-38

Located across the street from the Laguna Vista Lodge Historic Restaurant and Saloon is the Eagle Nest Café, which is now a restaurant but was once one of the most popular gambling dens in Eagle Nest. The Eagle Nest Café seems to have inherited an unruly female neighbor who reportedly has a great hatred for men as they are her favorite target. Pots and pans, which seem to be this snarky spirit's weapon of choice, fly independently across the room. Many, mostly men, have reported being pranked by the angry spirit as they enter the front door of the Eagle Nest Café, which was, at one time, her front door.

LAS VEGAS

Called the "Wildest of the Wild" by author/historian Howard Bryan, Las Vegas puts her sister city of today in Nevada to shame with its antics in the 1870s and 1880s. Cattlemen, railroaders, soldiers, gamblers, outlaws, and shady ladies as well as a few good upstanding folks all called Las Vegas home and helped to form the town we know today. For anyone who loves history, Las Vegas is the place to go. With over four hundred homes on the historic register, you will be able to witness any style of architecture available during that time frame.

John Henry "Doc" Holliday, who had a dentist's office and saloon in town with his girlfriend, Mary Horony Cummings, otherwise known as Big Nose Kate, and his friend Wyatt Earp, once walked these historic streets. It is said Doc Holliday killed his first man in Las Vegas, in the street outside his saloon; he packed up soon after for Tombstone. If the streets could talk, a tale of terror they would tell.

Shootings and murder were commonplace in the small town and got so bad that the citizens put together a flyer and a vigilante committee to warn anyone with the intention of causing trouble that they would be dealt with immediately, most likely at the hanging windmill in the town plaza. Gangs such as the White Caps and the Silva Gang ruled Las Vegas with an iron fist and struck fear into its citizens.

BYRON T'S SALOON, HISTORIC PLAZA HOTEL 230 PLAZA STREET

Lovingly known as the Belle of the Southwest, the Historic Plaza Hotel has stood proud on the Las Vegas Plaza Park since 1882 when it was originally built for $25,000. As the fanciest hotel in the entire territory for its era, the Plaza Hotel is situated proudly as a cornerstone of the historic Las Vegas Plaza, now known as Plaza Park. The town of Las Vegas played host to those who were traveling the last leg of the Santa Fe Trail and was larger than both Albuquerque and Santa Fe in the 1880s.

At three stories, the Plaza Hotel features a Victorian facade that looks today much like what the travelers of the past would have encountered then. Described as looking "like a wedding cake" due to the fancy scrollwork around the windows and doors, the Plaza was proud to feature thirty-seven rooms, a saloon, a dance hall, and a restaurant. The rich walnut door frames, windowsills, and staircase have lasted the test of time, and her beauty has made the belle a movie star. If you look closely while watching *No Country for Old Men*, *Easy Rider*, the television series *Longmire*, or *Ransom Canyon*, you will recognize the Historic Plaza Hotel in the background or as a setting.

Many cattle and land deals have been made in the saloon, now known as Byron T's. Outlaws (most of whom were notorious), lawmen, salesmen, politicians, and presidents have walked through the fourteen-foot-tall glass doors of the Historic Plaza Hotel. Finely crafted floors and tilework grace the interior of the lobby, dining room, and saloon, much of which was done by highly talented New Mexican artists and craftsmen.

Meticulously restored, the Historic Plaza Hotel is listed on the National Register of Historic Places and is highly recommended as the first choice for lodging when you visit Las Vegas, New Mexico.

Haunted Tales

The ghost of Byron T. Mills, owner of the Historic Plaza Hotel in the early 1900s, has been reported to visit unsuspecting travelers in their rooms; he especially is fond of redheaded women who travel alone, or so the story goes. The author's encounter with this spirit is what started her on this haunted journey as she was a sceptic at first. Having been told "There's no such thing as ghosts" from childhood, it was a little unbelievable to her that such a thing

Known as the Belle of the Southwest, the stunning redbrick Plaza Hotel has been an anchor of the Las Vegas Plaza Park since 1882.

The reportedly haunted room of former owner Byron T. Mills is said to be one of the most photographed rooms in the Plaza Hotel.

could exist—even though she had felt the presence of something around her on many occasions in her youth.

After arriving in Las Vegas for a mini conference, she decided to put the rumors to the test and stay at the Historic Plaza Hotel to see for herself. The clean, sparsely appointed room contained a bed, a tall cabinet to be used as a closet, and a small table and chairs. She felt she was being watched from the start but dismissed this as her imagination—though it still made for an uncomfortable situation while she was taking a shower and dressing for dinner that evening.

While reviewing the information for the conference after dinner, she fell asleep with the light on, surrounded by conference pamphlets and papers. When she woke up a little later, she realized she needed to clean up the bed so she could get some rest for the next day, but as she attempted to turn over, she felt pressure in the small of her back, preventing her from moving. The terror response was immediate—but this is what she was testing, wasn't it?

After a few minutes of trying to regain her wits, she finally addressed the presence, saying aloud that she had a long day in the morning and could he please leave her alone. She was surprised at the immediate response as the pressure disappeared, as did the feeling of being watched.

A female ghost is also said to haunt the Historic Plaza Hotel, but not much is written about her presence. The smell of orange blossoms is her telltale sign, according to New Mexico paranormal author Cody Polston. A large stain on the hardwood floor at the foot of the stairs is covered by a rug; much speculation has people wondering if the stain could be the result of bloodshed.

Since Las Vegas utilized the base of a windmill located in the town plaza directly across from the Historic Plaza Hotel as a gallows, even for just one year, it's no wonder there are lingering spirits in the historic district.

CHAPTER 2
NORTHWEST AND CENTRAL REGIONS

NORTHWEST NEW MEXICO

CHAMA

Historic Foster's Hotel and Bar is located on Main Street in a picturesque setting surrounding the town of Chama, New Mexico. Only eight miles from the Colorado border, Chama is a railroad town, famous for the Cumbres & Toltec Scenic Railroad, a narrow-gauge railroad that travels sixty-four miles along some of the most beautiful scenery in New Mexico and Colorado, especially spectacular in the fall months. Touted as the "longest, highest and most authentic steam railroad in North America" on its website, this adventure is absolutely something to put on your bucket list.

Golden cottonwood trees that line the roads are a spectacle for the eyes as you drive into town in the fall at an elevation of 7,860 feet. Hunting, fishing, mountain biking, and hiking are available for those who like to play outdoors. Sargent's Wildlife Area includes expansive mountain meadows where you can go for a horseback ride should you desire. Winter sports such as snowmobiling and cross-country skiing complete the sports year. A beautiful RV park can accommodate your travel trailer should you have one in tow; please be sure to make reservations ahead of your arrival as slots fill up fast, especially in the fall. For those of you who enjoy the peacefulness of strolling in a quaint town, there are also many shops featuring locally crafted items and cafés available for your enjoyment.

Chama is a jewel in the fall as the cottonwoods begin to change to their golden coats, highlighting the local statuary at the train depot.

FOSTER'S HOTEL AND BAR
393 S. TERRACE AVENUE

Built in the late 1800s, Foster's Hotel and Bar has been a constant for Chama as it is the oldest commercial structure in town, having survived several fires that consumed most of the town, and has seen numerous owners and operators along the way. Many additions have allowed the building to grow to meet the needs of the railroad town, which once had only two hotels.

Haunted Tales

One of the most prevalent hauntings in Foster's involves the first female judge elected in the male-dominated Chama in the late 1800s, whose room was in the southwest corner of the upper floor of the hotel. One morning,

A survivor of several devastating fires that threatened to level Chama, Foster's Hotel and Bar has been a constant staple of the downtown landscape.

the judge was found dead in this room, and rumors about the cause began to fly. Poison was found in the pitcher of drinking water on her dresser, and the conclusion that held the most weight was traced back to a group of men from the town who were not in love with the idea of having a woman judge in their community. The sounds of a woman choking and gasping for air have been reported coming from the direction of the ill-fated judge's room. As was typical for the day, no one was ever tried for her death.

The spirits of a young girl who reportedly died of an illness in the hotel and a cowboy, possibly killed in the downstairs bar, have been seen and overheard through the years in the closed-off section of the second floor and the unfinished attic. The anguished cries of pain and calls for help from a little girl have been heard emanating from one of the rooms on the second floor, startling the hotel staff. Heavy footsteps that echo through the wooden floors to the rooms below as if made by cowboy boots, thought to be those of an unidentified railroad worker, make it sound as though a person is pacing around yet another room on the second floor.

Of course there are the typical reports of cold spots, orbs and brief "gusts of wind" in and around the affected areas of the upper floors. Not to be outdone, the newer section of Foster's also has its paranormal activity as well, Rooms 21 and 25 contain the most activity. A dark figure has been observed in Room 21, which disappears as it reaches the door. Room 25 has guests complaining of extreme fluctuations in heat and cold that last for several minutes. All these factors make Foster's Hotel and Bar a popular destination for ghost hunters. Ongoing investigations are being conducted to prove or debunk the validity of the numerous claims.

GALLUP

As the last New Mexico leg of the famed Route 66 going west and a gateway community to the state of Arizona, Gallup is known as the Indian Capital of the World as it is part of the Navajo Nation, the Adventure Capital of New Mexico, and the home of Red Rock Park. As a hub of the Native American cultural and art communities, Gallup is home to many Native artists who have graced the world with their intricate artwork, silver and turquoise jewelry, highly sought-after weaving, and fine pottery talents. Gallup prides itself on being home to the most authentic Native-made turquoise jewelry you will find in the nation.

A little-known fact is that during World War II, if it had not been for the Navajo language known and spoken by the Navajo code talkers from Gallup, it is highly likely the United States would not have won the war against Japan. The Navajo call themselves the Diné (which means the People); their language is highly complex and could not be broken by the Japanese code breakers. These code talkers had to translate a huge number of military terms into precise code in an extremely short period of time and do it perfectly for it to work. We as a nation have a huge debt to pay to the Navajo Nation as we relish our freedom today. The Navajo Code Talker Museum is a must-see when you visit Gallup. Other tribes whose members served as code talkers were the Choctaw, Comanche, and Meskwaki—our greatest appreciation to them as well. We must never forget their efforts and sacrifices.

Stunning landscapes surround Gallup as red sandstone monuments rise out of the desert to greet you. Hiking, biking, fishing, birdwatching, and fabulous opportunities for photography abound around the town of Gallup. Each year a hot air balloon festival is held using the breathtaking red rocks as a backdrop; it is a sight to experience at least once.

EL RANCHO HOTEL/SILVER SCREEN CAFÉ/49ER LOUNGE 1000 E. HIGHWAY 66

"Charm of yesterday and convenience of tomorrow" is on the sign that greets your arrival at El Rancho Hotel. Ever wonder where John Wayne, Kirk Douglas, Ronald Reagan, Jane Wyman, Gregory Peck, Errol Flynn, Katherine Hepburn, and Spencer Tracy, plus many more, stayed while filming the epic Westerns of their day while in New Mexico? The historic El Rancho Hotel in Gallup, New Mexico, of course. This 1940s architectural masterpiece has been a haven for many of the Hollywood elite as they brave the red desert sands and heat surrounding Gallup to make their unforgettable movies. Rubbing elbows with the Duke was commonplace at the El Rancho Hotel, which was designed by a twenty-one-year-old architect from England. Gallup is still used today as a beautiful backdrop for television series, such as the popular *Dark Winds*.

Most of the rooms at the hotel still bear the names of the stars who stayed in them during the Western era. One of the more interesting pieces of memorabilia is the original shovel used to break ground for El Rancho. It is dedicated to Lucien Maxwell, of Maxwell Land Grant fame, who was one of the largest landowners in the 1800s in northeastern New Mexico.

Corrals were in the rear of the property for the actor's mounts. One amusing story from that era occurred when actor Errol Flynn rode his horse back to the hotel after a particularly hot and dusty day of filming—but instead of stopping at the corrals, Flynn rode his steed into what is now the 49er Lounge and ordered himself a whiskey and a beer for his faithful

The iconic El Rancho Hotel was a respite for Hollywood actors and their crew as they frequented the area, filming their famous Westerns.

horse. Not to be outdone, when John Wayne heard of Flynn's stunt, he did the same. It is said this story was the inspiration for the Toby Keith/Willie Nelson collaboration "Beer for My Horses." Actor/singer Dean Martin was once thrown off the balcony by a jealous husband after Martin apparently serenaded the man's wife.

One tour around Gallup and the surrounding landscapes and you will know why El Rancho Hotel was the right choice for those in the past and yourself today.

Haunted Tales

Although some do not want to speak of the otherworldly happenings at El Rancho Hotel, others have stated the structure is highly haunted by playful spirits who like to turn off music.

The woman in white also makes an appearance at the hotel; she is seen flowing down the magnificent wooden staircase in the center of the hotel lobby. The lady has also been seen slamming the door to the bridal suite on occasion. A woman screaming is sometimes heard by the night desk clerks, which makes for a long night.

Pots and pans in the kitchen have been seen slamming against one another in the early morning hours before the cooks arrive. Reports of a presence being felt in the kitchen have staff avoiding being in the area alone.

SOCORRO

Centrally located, Socorro has been a hub for the cattle industry and mining operations since its inception in 1626 with the establishment of the Nuestra Señora de Perpetuo Mission. At the end of the Jornada De Muerto (Dead Man's Journey) and El Camino Real (Royal Highway), which was the route settlers from Mexico would take to come into the interior of New Spain, Socorro was established as a place of rest. The name Socorro means "aid" or "help." During the Pueblo Revolt of 1680, Socorro was a place of refuge for the Spanish settlers who were fleeing the northern settlements on their way to El Paso, Texas. The region was not resettled until 1692.

Silver and gold mines are prevalent in the Magdalena Mining District, which includes the mountains surrounding Socorro. It was rumored so much silver was taken from this district (approximately 786,000 ounces) that the altar railing for the Catholic church was made from pure silver. This railing was removed and buried for protection from theft during the Pueblo Revolt of 1680, never to be seen again. So many minerals and gems were mined from the region that Socorro was soon dubbed the Gem City. Today, Socorro is home to the New Mexico Institute of Mining and Technology, which educates some of the most brilliant minds in the world. Copper, manganese, gold, zinc, and lead have been mined from the district, making this one of the richest mining regions in the country during its heyday.

Socorro has seen its share of troubles as well, being the stomping grounds for the likes of cattle thief and murderer Joel Fowler and the alleged female serial killer "Bronco Sue" Yonkers. The small town has seen many citizens' group lynchings mainly performed by the Socorro Vigilantes from the old cottonwood trees as well as many sensational trials featuring the alluring Bronco Sue.

Today, Socorro offers many activities to the traveler. It is a few miles southwest of the Trinity Site, the location of the first atomic bomb tests. The Karl G. Jansky Very Large Array Radio Telescopes, west of Socorro,

Socorro, which means "help," is at the end of El Camino Real and was a welcome sight for those who traveled there from Mexico City.

were featured in the movie *First Contact*; visitors are given up close and personal access to the huge satellite dishes being used by scientist to listen for life elsewhere. You will be close to historical sites such as Fort Craig, an American Civil War fort only a few miles down the road. And for the birdwatchers out there, the Bosque del Apache National Wildlife Refuge provides a wonderful experience when the sandhill cranes arrive in the fall. Rockhounding and rock-climbing opportunities abound in the surrounding region, where massive coal mines once operated.

CAPITOL BAR & BREWERY
110 PLAZA STREET

The Capitol Bar & Brewery sits in a prominent spot on the southeast corner of the Socorro Plaza in historic downtown Socorro. It started life as just one of many bars in town; it is said there was a bar on every corner. The original saloon was owned by the Italian immigrant Giovanni Biavaschi and his family, who built the two-story brick structure on the southeast corner of the plaza in 1896. At the time of its construction, the Biavaschis promised this building would "last the ages"—which it has, as it is Socorro's only remaining saloon from the territorial era.

When the Biavaschi family was unable to keep the saloon due to unforeseen circumstances, it became the Club Bar under the ownership of Judge Amos Green. Later it become the Torres and Gallegos Bar under the management of former Socorro Mayor José K. Torrez and his business partner Pete Gallegos. Prohibition hit the region hard, but this bar survived as it was turned into a pool hall instead. A fire that nearly burned down the entire historic plaza in 1923 was almost the undoing of the establishment. Today, the plaza is restored and is still a vibrant part of the community as it hosts many events throughout the year, and the Capitol Bar & Brewery patio is a great place to drink in the ambiance of the town.

The Capitol Bar & Brewery is an 1896 two-story brick structure located on the southeastern corner of the town plaza and has witnessed much history.

After Prohibition ended in 1933, Fred Emilio obtained Socorro's first liquor license, and the saloon was later known as the Green Front Saloon in honor of the late Judge Green, who owned this and other bars from 1909 until his death in 1925. According to family members, Emilio insisted on stocking the finest whiskey and "refused to handle the cheap stuff." Fred Emilio was a practical man who hung a sign in his saloon that read, "If your money is needed at home, don't spend it here." No word on whether the regulars took these words to heart.

Haunted Tales

The stone-walled cellar was accessible from the main building of the oldest saloon in the state by a trapdoor behind the bar. Down there, liquor supplies were hidden from Prohibition agents. Rumor also has it that a professor at New Mexico Tech taught some students in the basement; it is said the students were actually digging a tunnel from the Capitol Bar to the campus. Unfortunately for the students, this tunnel was never completed. Apparitions of what are thought to be former students have been seen and heard in this failed tunnel area.

Outlaw and murderer Joel Fowler met his death at the end of a rough rope in the Socorro Plaza after he brutally murdered a salesman while deep in his cups. Townsfolk had become fed up with the violent behavior of some residents and formed a vigilante group, which effectively took care of the situation when the lawmen's hands were tied by red tape. Fowler's last minutes were spent begging to live, and some say his ghost still wanders the plaza and frequents the Capitol Bar & Brewery.

CENTRAL NEW MEXICO

ALBUQUERQUE

As New Mexico's largest city, Albuquerque had grown significantly from its early days as just a few streets of adobe huts. With growth comes progress, and this can have both good and bad effects. The amount of time it takes to get across the city is immense, especially for someone who comes from a much smaller town, but the opportunities Albuquerque offers outweigh the inconveniences of heavy traffic. No matter what you need, rest assured, Albuquerque can provide.

Like the rest of the state, Albuquerque has an old and storied past filled with turmoil and upheaval. Highly influenced by Mexican and Spanish culture, it has been dubbed the Duke City due to its namesake, Viceroy Francisco Fernández de la Cueva, the Tenth Duke of Albuquerque. The town has also been known as Alburquerque (the extra *r* was later dropped). This rapidly growing town saw an insurgence of the Anglo culture with the arrival of the railroad in 1870s. Today, the city is a medley of nearly every race and nationality on earth, which brings richness to Albuquerque society.

If you plan on visiting Albuquerque, please take advantage of all it has to offer, ranging from hiking, biking, zoos, botanical gardens, ancient petroglyphs, kayaking, casinos, theater, sporting events, trams, and, of course, the world-famous International Balloon Fiesta, which occurs in the first week of October. A word to the wise: If you are planning to come for the fiesta, make your reservations as early as possible. Hotel prices will double, if not triple, the closer you get to the event since it attracts literally thousands of tourists to the city and competition is high for the limited amount of hotel rooms available.

ALBUQUERQUE PRESS CLUB
201 HIGHLAND PARK CIRCLE SE

Open any reference book concerning haunted places in Albuquerque and you will encounter the Albuquerque Press Club first—not just because of the alphabetical aspect but also because the large log cabin that overlooks its close neighbor, the Hotel Parq Central (which is also highly haunted), has a long-standing reputation for being haunted as there have been reports of a woman in white walking on the roof. Built in 1903 as a private residence, the sturdy building eventually became the members-only clubhouse it is today with stunning views of the historic district of old Albuquerque.

The rustic cabin structure is a little out of place next to the more modern buildings that surround the parklike locale. This small patch of trees and green grass provides those who find their way to the doorstep of the Albuquerque Press Club with a sense of peace as the city's craziness seems

New Mexico's largest city is a melting pot of every culture you can imagine and celebrates each with the honor and respect it deserves.

The log cabin Albuquerque Press Club was once located in a suburban area of the city but today it is surrounded by its modern neighbors.

to melt away. It's no wonder the club was and is a favorite of leaders in the media. Being able to relax on the front veranda with your favorite beverage and enjoying the lights of the city below is quite a draw. The front entry to the club is paved with bricks bearing the names of local television and radio stations as well as local media celebrities.

The Albuquerque Press Club overlooks one of the most haunted hotels in Albuquerque: the Hotel Parq Central. It was built in 1926 and served as a hospital for the Atchison, Topeka & Santa Fe Railroad until the 1980s, when it became a mental health facility for troubled teens. This striking building is now one of Albuquerque's most luxurious hotels and features the stunning Apothecary Rooftop Lounge, which has breathtaking views of Albuquerque. When visiting the Albuquerque Press Club, take a tour of this neighboring property, which may just share the spirits of its past occupants.

Haunted Tales

An apparition known as Mrs. M seems to be the most-sighted ghost of the Albuquerque Press Club. Arriving in Albuquerque in 1916 from Louisiana, Mrs. M was a caregiver for a tuberculosis patient who came to the state for the drier climate. The tuberculosis sanitarium was located at what is now the Hotel Parq Central, which is also extremely haunted. It is said that by 1920, the Albuquerque Press Club had become Mrs. M's home. She told her first husband, pharmacist A.B. Hall, she would only marry him if he bought the "house on the hill" (the Press Club log cabin), which she had fallen in love with most. He did.

Mrs. M also used the log cabin's lay-in porch as a recovery place for her patients, some from the nearby pueblos. Unfortunately, some of them did not survive their battle with the terrible disease. Mrs. M opened her home to artists and writers, and soon it was filled to the brim with Native American art and world treasures. Interestingly, the log cabin was also the site of her and Mr. Hall's bathtub gin distillery during Prohibition, where they distilled gin and brewed beer for bottling—but her daughter, Mary Lou Heaphy, says Mrs. M enjoyed bourbon the most.

Mrs. M's real name is Clifford (because her father wanted a boy) Myrick Hall McCallum. A photo in the Press Club shows Mrs. M as a tall brunette with a stern face, sporting a dark cape—which matches the description of the most-seen apparition.

A woman dressed in a dark cloak is often seen standing next to the bar, staring. This is unsettling for the bar staff, who witness her from time to time. One of Mrs. M's tricks is playing a few notes on the piano in the main room. This action even draws the attention of the resident cat, who sits and stares off into space—at nothing. Staff swear they can hear the clacking of the nurse's heels on the wooden floors when it is quiet enough in the room. Mrs. M's presence is felt rather than seen lately.

After two divorces, Mrs. M stayed in her beloved home for forty years until 1960, when she could no longer take care of the magnificent home. Mrs. M passed away shortly thereafter from cancer at the age of eighty-seven and is buried in the Fairview Memorial Park.

There are tales of bartenders from many years ago leaving a jigger of liquor on the bar for the gin-loving ghost and finding the glass empty by morning. Could Mrs. M still be enjoying her traditional gin?

CASA VIEJA BREWERY
4541 CORRALES ROAD

Known as a one-of-a-kind destination, Casa Vieja (which translates to "Old House") in historic Corrales, New Mexico (a suburb of Albuquerque), is owned by native New Mexicans and proudly serves its own craft beer and exclusive Viñedo Pajaro Azed wines from a former adobe home that was built in 1770. Drink in the atmosphere and the spirits in the taproom or on the spacious patio, where live music is played most nights of the week. Food trucks provide local fare and offer brewery patrons the total package.

Corrales is a unique horse community filled with wineries and vineyards. You can visit the farmer's markets on the weekends and the numerous festivals that are held throughout the year. Casa Vieja Brewery is a vital part of this community vibe.

Casa Vieja was originally built as a home by Salvador Martinez on Alameda Land Grant land, and the property has been home to a French nunnery, a courthouse, a jail, a soldiers' barracks, and a mercantile. Trials were held in the oldest part, and if the accused was found guilty, they were taken to the hanging tree on Corrales Road to be pelted by rotten vegetables—depending on the severity of the crime. Over the years, the home began to decline due to hardships in the 1930s and World War II, but the Harrington family from Sioux City, Iowa, purchased it in 1941 and immediately began restoration to preserve the original integrity of the adobe structure. Additions were made over the years, such as kiva fireplaces, nichos, built-in bookcases, flagstone and brick floors. After Tom and his wife, Dorothy, who was the first to call their home Casa Vieja (the Old House), divorced in 1950, Casa Vieja was sold to Dr. Alan Jacobson, who converted the expanded building into a small psychiatric hospital to serve the community.

The Bentley family gained ownership in the 1970s and converted the hospital into a fine dining establishment. The Socha family, Gary and Linda, were next in line to own the historic building; they purchased it in 2016. It was then that Casa Vieja was born and became the brewery we know today, now owned by Daniel O'Brien and his wife, Molly Smith. Casa Vieja is on the New Mexico State Register of Cultural Properties and is honored to display a plaque from the Corrales Historical Society that proclaims the rich history of the building, which is in the heart of Corrales. It is said that during a remodeling session by the Bentleys, a hidden painting was found within one of the building's walls in the newest part of the building. This painting of a French duke inspired the Duke's Red Ale brewed on-site. Also featured is a Ghost Stout, made from light grains, which "resembles a chocolate stout."

Haunted Tales

Paranormal teams have visited Casa Vieja over the years, inspiring the Ghost Stout's name. Strains of a little girl singing in French can be heard which can be nice but unsettling for some. Orbs have been caught on infrared cameras. The current owners state these lively spirits are good for business since they are not menacing and add a certain ambiance to the Casa Vieja experience. In any hospital setting, there will be lingering spirits, but these seem to be keen on having a good time.

Recent ghost-hunting ventures have experienced evidence of memories, such as the voice of a child looking for her grandparents. A local psychic, Cynthia Hess, stated there are numerous spirits and energies attached to the building; some came for healing and rest in the past and never left since they felt at home. The presence of a frail woman is felt. She seems to feel responsible for keeping the kitchen going as she used to work in the home. The adobe, being an earthen vessel of sorts, seems to hold memories. A voice was captured during one paranormal session. A woman carrying geraniums in the dining room was seen by a server, although there was no one else in the building.

Former owner Linda Socha experienced several paranormal occurrences during her time. Doors opened and closed by themselves; even a spring-loaded door opened on its own. The sounds of a commotion were startling to her, at first, but she became used to such activity. Art shows seem to bring out activity from the spirits, according to former owners.

Legends of a body, or two, being found in the walls of Casa Vieja linger. According to one story, two monks dressed in purple robes with gold crucifixes were found embedded in the oldest part of the building. The theory is that since Corrales flooded quite often, the nearby church buried people under the floor in the church instead of in the cemetery; the monks may have been buried in the wall during the late 1770s. There is also the story of a golden Madonna being added to a wall in the oldest part of the building; it has not yet been found. A recently found keystone seems to point toward the wall.

The voice of a little girl, possibly speaking French, has been heard during EVP sessions; it answered many questions from the team. Some of the voices, thought to emanate from the nunnery or psychiatric hospital, have stunned investigators. One of the former owners from 1941, Tom Harrington, reported dancing with an enchanting entity named Lucille, to whom he would bring flowers. One of the last flowers he brought was left on a windowsill and retained its color for years.

Without a doubt, from the investigative result perspective alone, Casa Vieja Brewery is the place to go if you want a ghostly experience.

OLD TOWN ALBUQUERQUE

The Plaza of Old Town Albuquerque has been the site of great celebrations and great tragedies and is thought to be highly haunted by multiple ghosts. It would be quite a ruckus if the Civil War captain, the woman wielding a hatchet, and the lady of the night showed up at the same time.

Nearly every weekend, the Old Town Plaza can be found filled with an impromptu car show featuring some of Albuquerque's most impressive lowriders. These beautiful vehicles are generally crafted from cars ranging from the 1950s to present-day models, elaborately decorated, painted, and pinstriped with highly reflective metal-flake paint and fitted with their signature special hydraulic suspension systems. The prized original vehicles

Old Town Plaza of Albuquerque is the city's oldest neighborhood; legends and lore surround every one of the ancient adobe structures in its midst.

can be raised and lowered at the wheels either collectively or independently at the whim of the driver or even bounced for the thrill of passengers and observers alike.

Weddings, quinceañeras, concerts, and rallies are commonplace in the historic plaza and can be enjoyed by all as you stroll through the many wonderful shops around the square. The star of the plaza must be San Felipe de Neri Catholic Church on the north end, with its towering spires and adobe architecture. Before the plaza existed as we know it today, the grounds in front of the church were used as the cemetery until floods began to destroy the sacred grounds. As a result of the floodwaters, many graves were opened and the bodies were displaced, leaving the town without a clue about to whom the skeletal remains belonged. It was decided the bones would be collected and placed for safekeeping in the left spire of the church, where they remain today.

CHURCH STREET CAFÉ
2111 CHURCH STREET NW

Since starting out as an eighteen-room hacienda, the over-three-hundred-year-old structure, built in 1709, that's now known as the Church Street Café has lived a long and sometimes troubled life, surviving floods, neglect, and the real threat of simply melting away since it was constructed of adobe. The old building, known as Casa De Ruiz, needed a hero, who came in the unlikely form of college student Marie Coleman. Coleman noticed the derelict building, saw its potential, and was somehow drawn to help it survive in 1993.

Tucked into a narrow roadway behind San Felipe de Neri Church, the iconic Church Street Café offers over four generations of New Mexico cuisine experience to local and visiting customers. Due to the narrowness of the road in front of the café, and the "no parking" signs, it is highly recommended you use one of the public parking lots located around the Old Town area. Make sure you pay your lot fee, or you will be quickly ticketed.

The Church Street Café was a private residence until the death of Rufina G. Ruiz in 1991. When Marie Coleman gained ownership, she decided to

Once a private residence, the Church Street Café is haunted by the former owner, Sarah Ruiz, who is still protecting her precious adobe home.

renovate and preserve the building. This is when the new owner began to receive messages in the terrifying form of disembodied screams to get rid of the contractor. Not to be dissuaded from his job, the contractor began to build a rapport with the spirit, who continually moved his tools, buckets, and supplies. The spirit was thought to be that of Rufina's mother, Sara Ruiz, who apparently was not too happy with the changes being made in her home. On several occasions, the contractor had to ask Marie Coleman to please tell the ghost to let him work and leave his tools alone. After Marie spoke heart to heart with Sara, the occurrences seemed to minimize.

Haunted Tales

Stories of the former owner—the petite, white-haired Sara Ruiz—haunting the Church Street Café have circulated for many years. The lady has definite ideas about how her home is used and how the food is prepared in this, one of Albuquerque's oldest establishments. This home remained under the loving embrace of the Ruiz family for three centuries; Juliana Ruiz (Sara's daughter) was its last resident. Providing solace for family and visitors alike, the Church Street Café became a hub for local meetings and festive gatherings.

Dolls and, especially, the pink trinkets displayed in cases in the café's front lobby reportedly move or are in different spots when the staff opens the restaurant in the morning. Those who forget to tell Señora Ruiz good night at the end of the evening have reported feeling the woman's presence following them home. Sara has also been known to turn the lights of the restaurant back on after the last staff member had closed for the evening, leading to some frustration, especially after an especially busy evening of serving guests.

One frightening occurrence was reported by staff and patrons alike: They all found themselves lined up along the adobe walls as silverware and knives played in the air on all the tables in front of them. Keys have been known to vanish without a trace only to reappear far across the room after the person looking for them apologized to Sara for their transgression. The heavy wooden doors of the café have been known to slam shut on their own power without any draft of air coming into play.

LA PLACITA DINING ROOMS/OLD TOWN CAFÉ/ CASA DE ARMIJO 206 SAN FELIPE STREET NW

Housed in the Casa de Armijo building on the southeastern corner of the Old Town Plaza, La Placita Dining Rooms (*la placita* means "little square") can boast of being in one of the oldest buildings in New Mexico, dating back over three hundred years. It, like many of the other structures on the Plaza, used to be a personal home—in this case, belonging to Don Ambrosio Armijo.

Armijo ran a general store out of the lower floor of the Pueblo Revival–style structure, while the upper floor served as the family residence. It was also used as a hotel before being converted into a restaurant in 1931; the dining room opened in 1935. One of the building's most unique features was kept: the ancient cottonwood tree that grows out of the center of the dining room. An elaborate staircase that was imported from Spain graces the entryway.

Known for its delicious New Mexican fare, La Placita was steadily busy as the aromas of the roasted chiles and fajitas tempted visitors to come inside from the heat or cold of the plaza. Heavily renovated in the 1970s—renovations are known to stir up ghosts—La Placita continued in business until 2022, when the strain of the COVID-19 era took its final toll.

Now known as the Old Town Café, the restaurant still carries on some of the traditions of the original owners although it is mainly a sandwich shop today.

Haunted Tales

La Placita Dining Rooms is reportedly haunted by four spirits who like to give the restaurant patrons a little something extra with their meal: a side of fright.

There are reports of visitors seeing the face of a young girl, about six years old, peering back at them when they look into the vanity mirrors in the lady's restroom. Historic records state a young girl did pass away in 1880 in the house at a young age. The restroom was once a part of the girl's bedroom. This same girl, whose name was Maria, is also seen playing in the dining room under the tables and running around the room in a pink dress.

The aroma of roasted green chiles tempts passersby to come inside La Placita Dining Room to enjoy a wonderful meal of traditional New Mexico cuisine.

Maria was the favorite granddaughter of Don Armijo and liked to play in the building as a child. Tragically, Maria became very sick and passed away around her sixth birthday. It is thought Maria's love for her grandfather was so strong that she did not want to leave his side. Since Don Armijo's death, patrons and staff have reported seeing the old man bouncing young Maria on his knee. The main stairwell leading to the second-floor residence was a favorite area for young Maria to play, so it makes sense that people report seeing the child playing there or walking through the walls to find her favorite spot.

A woman dressed in black is sometimes observed walking the property carrying a baby. This is thought to be a woman named Victoriana who died in the building during childbirth. It is unknown if the baby survived.

Restaurant staff have heard "strange whispers" and experienced multiple cold spots while working upstairs. The kitchen staircase is another hot spot of activity; staff members have noticed shadow figures and unexplained fog or mist.

A little girl in a communion dress floating down the exquisite staircase has been seen as well. Her dress is covered in white sun wheels inserted in the intricate beadwork. Traditionally a Navajo directional symbol used in blanket weaving and clothing, the sun wheel is sometimes confused with the German swastika.

HIGH NOON RESTAURANT & SALOON 425 SAN FELIPE STREET NW

The quaint adobe building on the corner of San Felipe and Mountain Road was built in the 1750s, which makes the High Noon one of the oldest buildings in Albuquerque, giving it great historical value.

The High Noon has a colorful past: It once served as a brothel and quickly became the favorite watering hole of every gambler, outlaw, and shady character in the territory. Oddly enough, due to its proximity to the Catholic church, the building also served as an apartment for nuns. Being such a rowdy place, the building was witness to many gunfights and murders stemming from losses at the gambling tables. All these events make for restless spirits.

Known for its delectable steaks and local cuisine, the High Noon Restaurant & Saloon is a favorite with tourists and Burqueños alike. This authentic New Mexican restaurant has established itself in the fascinating history of Old Town and Albuquerque. Be aware that the doorways of these historical structures were likely built to accommodate people of smaller stature than we have today; anyone six feet tall or taller will have to bend down to enter the Santos Room for that reason.

The Santos Room pays homage to the Spanish heritage of the region and is decorated with statuary and symbolism of that culture. The Kiva Room features high ceilings and thick adobe walls and is decorated with many spectacular examples of traditional Native American artwork such as Hopi kachinas, Navajo rugs, and Acoma pottery. The Gallery Room, also referred to as the Gringo Room, features black-and-white photographs of the historical progression of the adobe structure through its renovation.

Relying heavily on tourist traffic, the High Noon Restaurant & Saloon delivers those following the Margarita Trail a variety of over thirty tequilas

Rumors of the High Noon Restaurant & Saloon being haunted have proven to be true; the building has played host to gunfights and brothels.

to choose from for this favorite Old Town drink. Its food is described as "new food from the Old West" and is sure to have something for everyone's palette, from appetizers to delectable steaks. The Ancho BBQ Short Ribs are highly recommended by the staff.

Haunted Tales

One of the most consistent stories connected to the High Noon generally plays out in the Santos Room (a *santos* is a painted wooden panel, generally decorated with images of various patron saints). A woman respectfully referred to as the Lady in the White Dress is often seen in this room by those sensitive to such matters.

Unexplained noises, such as laughter and glasses clinking, are heard, keeping staff and patrons on edge, especially when they witness a piece of barware slide across the bar and levitate without any assistance. The High Noon seems to be harboring quite a bit of residual energy from its raucous past, often described as echoes—all of which seem to enjoy clinking glassware.

An apparition of a cowboy affectionately named the Gambler is said to like to join in on poker nights, making himself at home at the table. Shady ladies whose shrill laughter cuts through the quiet night also grace the historic restaurant. The pool table attracts most ghostly specters, such as the Gambler, who is reportedly seen sitting on or by the edge of this table participating in an eternal game of pool.

PAINTED LADY BED & BREW
1100 BELLAMAH AVENUE NW

When asked where the most haunted place in Old Town is located, my response is always Painted Lady Bed & Brew. While writing my book *Haunted Hotels and Ghostly Getaways*, I met the Lady's owner, Jesse Herron. The Lady was the establishment needed for the book that made publishing possible. Since that time, I can proudly say I have forged a lifelong friendship with him.

The Painted Lady offers a wealth of history, intrigue, and mystery. The series of buildings that comprise the complex held a myriad of enterprises over the years of their existence. They contained Charlie's Grocery Store, the Swastika Saloon, a brothel—and now a wonderfully haunted "bed and brew."

Located in the more industrial section of the Old Town community, just east of the plaza, the Painted Lady has seen its share of crazy characters and tragic events. When I asked Jesse about the paranormal occurrences he has experienced at the Lady, I was told tales (which I reveal most of in the following pages) that made my hair stand on end and, in some cases, truly made me shudder. As the scene of a brutal axe murder, the Lady has received menacing unwanted guests and evil entities who proved to be difficult to exorcise.

Shortly after purchasing the Lady, Jesse received a box of papers and documents that contained information about the building's sordid past. The person who gave it to him casually stated that Sheriff Pat Garrett and the famous outlaw Billy the Kid were once guests during their visit to Albuquerque on their way to Santa Fe. Jesse has not yet been able to find confirmation of the last claim, but it's certainly a fun theory to explore.

Jesse has developed a wonderful enterprise on Bellamah Avenue, which includes an authentic Albuquerque trolley car that now functions as the

One of the most haunted locations in Albuquerque is the Painted Lady Bed and Brew, which serves great ghost stories with its craft beers.

Experience a beautifully restored relic of the Old West, rumored to have been visited by none other than Pat Garrett and Billy the Kid.

Lady's brewery, where Jesse serves his very own craft beers, and an event space, which is used regularly for weddings, book signings, and ghost story sessions and lives up to its full potential especially during the spooky season in October. Featuring a ghost hunter's package that includes a night's stay in the Lizzie McGrath room, the use of an EMF meter during your stay, and a signed copy of my *Haunted Hotels and Ghostly Getaways*, the Painted Lady Bed & Brew is a full haunted package experience, not to be missed, and the Lady and its owner Jesse are true Old Town treasures.

Haunted Tales

As the Lady is in the Sawmill District and there's a large sawmill directly across the street, its time as a brothel was busy and raucous. The doors to the small cribs (rooms) of the ladies of the night faced toward the mill, which gave these ladies plenty of opportunities to tempt the workers to spend their hard-earned money with them instead of taking it home.

One of these ladies may have been working there to escape a controlling husband or attempting to make enough money to start fresh somewhere else. In any case, the man in her life was not pleased with her decision when he discovered his wayward wife in the arms of another man. After obtaining an axe, the husband returned and proceeded to unceremoniously hack the couple to death in the room that would become the owner's future apartment. Jesse reported he would sometimes be awakened by bloodcurdling screams.

The Painted Lady Bed and Brew has been a grocery store, brothel, and saloon in its lifetime and now play host to live entertainment weekly.

During his renovation of the former brothel, Jesse reported being visited by a tall, shadowy figure in a black hat that lurked in the corner of the owner's apartment. Thinking he had struck a bargain with the figure—I'll leave you alone if you leave me alone—Jesse went about his business until the entity began to torture his three-legged dog named Murray (yes, he was named after the actor Bill Murray). This proved to be too much to ignore and handle, and Jesse was forced to address the obvious elephant in the room. Paranormal experts were called in to alleviate Murray's anguish using spirit boxes, and sage cleanses, which seemed to work to remove the evil entity, at least temporarily.

Visitations from a particularly aggressive female succubus and the return of the evil entity unnerved the owner to the point that he decided to move away from the site. These have since been exorcised from the property and pose no threat to visitors.

During renovation, a large area of dark discoloration was discovered on the floor of one of the soon-to-be-rented rooms. Had there been another murder committed? Jesse is not sure, but it adds to the ambiance and theme of the Painted Lady perfectly. Embracing the "shady lady" brothel theme, each room is named for a famous lady of the night from Albuquerque—for example, Lizzie McGrath.

Lizzie was one of Albuquerque's richest madams; her brothel, the Vine Cottage, was located only a few blocks away from the Painted Lady as the crow flies. Lizzie was tough, savvy, and smart and was the only madam ever taken to the New Mexico Territorial Supreme Court for attempting to open a house of ill repute within seven hundred feet of a fraternal organization. Lizzie lost but created great newspaper fodder. Legend has it that Lizzie died of a heart attack while standing in line at the bank waiting to deposit her ill-gotten gains. But in stereotypical tradition—that is, the "hooker with a heart of gold"—Lizzie was also a great benefactor for the community, especially the children. The madam lent her last name to many of the orphans of the growing town. Today, you will notice many Hispanic McGraths in the area.

Jesse told me a story about Charlie, the owner of the grocery store. It appears he's still on duty checking the doors of the brothel. The jingle of his keys can be distinctly heard as he shuffles along the portico, checking each door on his way. Charlie is harmless as he continues to check on his property.

LOS LUNAS

LUNA MANSION/SPIRIT LOUNGE
123 MAIN STREET SW

This stately two-story Southern Colonial–style mansion located in the middle of modern-day Los Lunas, on the main street of town, is the town's best-known landmark but looks out of place against the territorial and adobe buildings that surround it, although it is said adobe was used in its construction as well.

The Luna-Otero Mansion belonged to the Lunas and the Oteros, founding families dating to 1692, when both became wealthy through land acquisitions and livestock. The two powerful families combined with the marriages of Solomon Luna to Adelaide Otero as well as Manuel A. Otero to Eloisa Luna in the late 1800s. This formed what was known as the Luna-Otero dynasty. The mansion served as a private residence for many years.

When the Atchinson, Topeka, and Santa Fe railroad needed the Luna-Otero land for its right-of-way through the land in 1880, it offered to build Antonio José Luna and his family this magnificent mansion in accordance with their wishes in return for the usage of their land. The mansion was completed in 1881; unfortunately for Antonio José, this was also the year of his death, so he could not enjoy the home. Antonio's eldest son, Tranquilino, and his family were the first to take possession. When Tranquilino died in 1892, his younger brother Solomon gained ownership.

By the early 1900s, the home had changed hands again, this time to Solomon's nephew, Eduardo Otero, since Solomon was childless. It was then that the renovations to the home began, which included a solarium, an ornate ironwork fence surrounding the entire property, and a front portico

Located in the heart of Los Lunas, the Luna Mansion has a reputation for being very haunted—and the place to get a great steak.

to grace the appearance of the already beautiful structure. Eduardo and his wife, Josefita—who was the daughter of William R. Manderfield, the founder of the *Santa Fe New Mexican* newspaper, lovingly known as Pepe—added the greatest amounts of improvements to the property during their time at the mansion. Josefita loved gardening, and the property grounds certainly benefited from her great attention.

After Eduardo's and Josefita's deaths, the mansion had several more owners and was turned into a fine dining establishment in the 1970s.

Haunted Tales

One of the main tales of haunting stems from the frequent sightings of Josefita, whose favorite chair, at the top of the stairs under her portrait, rocks independently of anyone sitting on it. An image of Josefita enjoying the chair has also been reported. An employee, not knowing the story, approached the lady sitting in the chair, but when he got close, the apparition stood up and vanished. Sightings of the lady of the house reportedly started in the 1970s when renovations began to turn her home into a restaurant. There are two trains of thought: Either Josefita did not like the renovations (renovations are usually when ghostly activity is at its highest), or she wanted to be there to supervise the work being done to her beloved home.

When she appears, Josefita is dressed in 1920s-style clothing, and she seems very real to the staff members who have seen her. The second-floor bedrooms, an attic storeroom, and the top of the stairs seem to be her favorite spots. Josefita has developed a habit of walking up and down the stairway that leads to the bar—she does this so much that the staff is used to the sight.

Another spirit acknowledged is thought to be that of a groundskeeper named Cruz. A jovial spirit, Cruz is said to be particularly fond of women and children and has been seen sitting on a sofa as though he is waiting to be served. Cruz is said to be a prankster and likes to play tricks on the unsuspecting staff.

Some have reported seeing visions of a Rough Rider, thought to be Maximillian Luna, and an image of a small boy who used to shine shoes at the mansion has been captured as well. Floors creak, and fleeting images are reported. It is heartbreaking to report that the Luna Mansion is currently looking for a new owner, but townspeople are hopeful the wonderful establishment will reopen soon.

MADRID

Coal was king in Madrid (pronounced *MAD-rid*), and with coal mining comes horrific mining accidents. Madrid did not escape, falling victim to some awful mining collapses and explosions. Evidence of mining operations can still be seen high on the hillsides surrounding the town in the form of tailings piles, rusted mining equipment, and abandoned miner shacks.

As a unique artist's community today, this town has something for everyone and can get quite busy during the summer months. It was Christmastime that brought attention to Madrid in the early days: The entire town would go all out in putting out Christmas lights everywhere, earning it the name Christmas Town. There were so many lights, in fact, that aircraft inbound to Albuquerque would make a special flyover of the town so their passengers could see the display.

As one of the locations for the 2007 movie *Wild Hogs*, starring John Travolta, Ray Liotta, Tim Allen, Marisa Tomei, Martin Lawrence, and William H. Macy, the small town was transformed and "discovered." You will recognize Maggie's Diner from the movie, which was built for the movie and never really was an eating establishment. Today, the "diner" is a T-shirt and memorabilia shop, a must-see when visiting. Shops along Main Street, which is Highway 14, also known as the Turquoise Trail, are brightly painted in various floral hues and lend a touch of whimsy for the eye—a photographer's paradise for sure.

The location of the Madrid Cemetery, which is as quirky as the town itself, is a highly guarded secret. But if you can somehow learn its location from one of the locals, it is well worth the extra effort to see. Please, please be respectful of the graves which are decorated in delightful ways. Each grave tells the life story of the person who is buried there and is quite touching to view. Don't be too disappointed if your request is refused; the cemetery is very special to the community. It is an honor to be given the knowledge.

Handmade crafts, locally sourced turquoise jewelry, and unique pieces of art that you may not be able to find anywhere else in the state can be found here in abundance in the quirky shops, opened in the once-humble miners' shacks that line the main street. Some of the turquoise fashioned into jewelry is from the still-active mines in the region, especially around the towns of Golden and Los Cerrillos up the road. Madrid is a mini Santa Fe in many ways, with the art scene so prevalent, but the town walks to the beat of its own drum. You almost expect a prospector to walk down the

Above: Madrid embraces and celebrates its dead; in fact, parties are held regularly at the town's unique and private cemetery, where each grave reflects its owner.

Opposite: Said to have the No. 1 Green Chile Cheeseburger in New Mexico, the Mineshaft Tavern in Madrid is the best haunted location to try this delicacy.

street with his trusty donkey or hear the end-of-the-day whistling from one of the coal mines. Take a minute to slow down and drink in the wonderful atmosphere of this fun and colorful hamlet.

MINESHAFT TAVERN
2864 NEW MEXICO 14

Settled at the edge of the art community of Madrid, the Mineshaft Tavern is a popular watering hole for tourists, bikers, and curiosity seekers along the famed Turquoise Trail on Highway 14. Since Madrid is a unique artist community, it is filled with larger-than-life personalities. In the warm months, the one-mile portion of Highway 14 that comprises Main Street Madrid is generally filled with tourists, motorcyclists, and buses, which vie for a prime parking spot on the narrow lane.

This traffic is good news for the Mineshaft Tavern, which relies on the summer months to survive. Established in 1899, the Mineshaft is a rustic setting in which to drink a cold beer on a hot summer day while experiencing the famous, award-winning delectable Mad Chile Burger, which was voted the No. 1 Green Chile Cheeseburger in New Mexico. For those of

you who don't know, this is the ultimate honor for a New Mexico green chile cheeseburger. Fine restaurants, burger joints, food trucks, and the like compete fiercely for this title. Freshly made pizza and sandwiches are also available along with child-friendly entrees.

Live music is a major draw for the Mineshaft Tavern, which brings in bands from all around the state and country to play every weekend and for special events during the year. You can enjoy your food and drink on the outdoor patio as well (weather permitting), where you'll have a bird's-eye view of the main road in and out of town.

Haunted Tales

Reports of the tavern doors opening and shutting of their own volition are commonplace at the Mineshaft Tavern. Bar patrons and staff have witnessed mysterious flying glasses that crash to the floor to shatter in a million pieces without help from patrons or staff. The distinctive sounds of a great celebration occurring when the saloon has been closed for a long time usually send new personnel looking for wayward customers, only to return empty-handed. One of the most disturbing ghostly actions happens in the restroom, where some have reported seeing another person's face staring back at them in the mirror.

Even the rest of town gets into the swing of things. A ghostly couple can often be seen strolling along Main Street, destination unknown. Halloween is a fantastic season to visit Madrid.

Images of men dressed in miner's garb carrying lunchboxes are seen on a regular basis; they just fit in with the vibe of the population and enjoy the atmosphere as they fade into the hillside.

CHAPTER 3
SOUTHEAST REGION

CARLSBAD

Positioned on the banks of New Mexico's second-largest river, the Pecos, Carlsbad began life as the town of Eddy in honor of its founder, Charles Bishop Eddy. Home to one of the largest irrigation projects in the United States, the fertile Pecos Valley had long been used as a standard for crop production in the state. Carlsbad straddles the Pecos River and is home to a variety of water sports, such as jet skiing, waterskiing, fishing, and boating. Paved walking trails flank the river's edge and provide a great source of exercise while visiting Carlsbad, which is nicknamed Cavern City.

Each year, beginning on Thanksgiving Day, the Pecos River comes alive as the beautiful homes along its banks present the world with light displays for Christmas on the Pecos. Barges and boats, piloted by the Carlsbad Navy, navigate the smooth waters of the Pecos so visitors can marvel at the beautiful Christmas presentations.

Twenty short miles away from the world-famous Carlsbad Caverns National Park, Carlsbad is thrilled to play host to multitudes of worldwide visitors who come to experience the phenomenal underground spectacle of the caverns. This is a must-see, bucket list item—truly a breathtaking sight that is beginning its second century of amazement. Please visit the historic restaurants mentioned here as you keep a keen eye out for the resident ghosts.

Be amazed by the wonderland located 750 feet under the desert landscape at the world-famous Carlsbad Caverns National Park, which just celebrated one hundred years of service.

Carlsbad is an industrial community: Mining and oil and gas are its main benefactors. Tourism dollars from Carlsbad Caverns National Park are also a welcome source of income for the Oasis on the Pecos. Another great site to visit during your stay is the Living Desert State Park, which is located on C Hill to the west of the town. This is a zoo and botanical park that features native plants and animals from the surrounding Chihuahuan Desert. The animals featured in the park have been rescued and cannot survive in the wild, so they are well cared for in the exhibits, which closely resemble their own habitats. It is best to visit the park early in the day to avoid the sometimes-intense desert heat.

LUCKY BULL GRILL AND SPORTS BAR 220 W. FOX STREET

The Lucky Bull Grill is in a building that started life as a fire station and has hosted several different businesses and restaurants during its lifespan. Once the new fire station was built, City Hall moved into the original brick structure. The author has a fond memory of going to the drive-in window with her mother to pay the water bill and being gifted the coins from the change, which were returned in little plastic bags. When City Hall moved one block away, it left the historical building empty for many years, although it was in a prime downtown location.

Eventually, in the late 1970s and early 1980s, a restaurant known as the Old City Hall opened, providing fine cuisine in a Victorian-style atmosphere complete with heavy burgundy drapes, a full mirrored bar backdrop made from mahogany downstairs, and a saloon setting upstairs. Today, the historic

Like other buildings in this book, the Lucky Bull Grill has worn many hats: a fire station, city hall, and various restaurants.

building is known as the Lucky Bull Grill and Sports Bar, which sports a large metal bull on its front entrance.

The bar is touted as an "American-style bar with a New Mexican twist." Local favorites include their steaks, Dirty Nachos, and green chile grits, and the specialty hamburgers are to die for. All these meals can be enjoyed with a New Mexico craft beer or popular favorites as well as local wine selections.

Haunted Tales

Staff members say the upstairs bar area and storage room are hot spots for ghostly activity. Several have reported being locked in the storeroom, which causes a great deal of anxiety for the staff. Glasses fly off the dry bar top without provocation, sometimes with napkins following. Servers have had their hair pulled and their names called. Strange noises and people talking have been heard emanating from the storeroom and the stairway leading to the bar upstairs.

THE TRINITY HOTEL & RESTAURANT
201 S. CANAL STREET

The stately Trinity Hotel & Restaurant is located in one of the few remaining historical buildings of its era left in Carlsbad, which started life as the First National Bank building circa 1892. Constructed from distinctive red brick in the popular Victorian architectural style, this proud lady was home to the offices of Charles B. Eddy and Sheriff Pat Garrett (of Billy the Kid fame) for a time as well as the home of the first newspaper printed in town and later became the offices of the Carlsbad Irrigation District.

Over the years, the CID building (as it was known locally) became dilapidated, and it was in danger of being torn down in 2007, but thanks to

Lovingly restored by the Balzano family, the Trinity Hotel & Restaurant serves up great food with a side of spirits when Ruby makes an appearance.

the Herculean efforts of the Balzano family and another investor, the old girl shines brightly. Under the close supervision of the New Mexico Historical Society, each phase of the restoration came one step closer to saving this beloved building. Today, the Trinity is well-known for its delicious food and wine, bringing a splendid touch of Italy to the New Mexico desert.

This exquisite boutique hotel features modern surfaces and conveniences housed in a historical shell. Whirlpool tubs, marble and glass showers, and flat-screen televisions and accessories are surrounded by period furniture and dark wood trim on the doors and windows, harking back to the time of the Trinity's construction. Wonderful aromas from the finest kitchen and dining room in Carlsbad will surely have you thanking your lucky stars for your choice of accommodation. Mimosas can be ordered with your morning meal, and some of the best wines grown in New Mexico, including the Trinity's own vineyard labels, can be enjoyed in the evenings—truly the best of both worlds.

Haunted Tales

An Arizona medium called her Ruby, and she is very possessive of her building. Long before the building housed the Trinity Hotel & Restaurant, it was the offices of the Carlsbad Irrigation District, and Ruby's office was on the second floor, where Room 206 is now. This lady ghost is also said to dislike women. Rumor has it Ruby was killed by a jealous wife, as reported by the Arizona medium, but this has not been proven. Ruby seems to be a prankster: She likes to turn off music, place towels on top of the high windowsills in her room, and, not so nicely, push female servers as they descend the steep stairs from the upper dining room. Servers have also reported hearing their name being called from time to time. A woman's face has been seen peering down from the second story, giving people who see her image a start.

Another more destructive spirit is aptly named the Glass Breaker by the staff. Witnesses report seeing glassware from the bar back and serving areas move on its own, only to crash into pieces on the original wooden floor. Be sure to ask your server for their personal account.

Trinity's vineyard is in the small town north of Carlsbad named Seven Rivers. This tiny community is basically a few buildings, a pecan orchard, and a small vineyard. The mile-long section of highway in front of Seven

Rivers is known as the most haunted mile of highway in New Mexico. State troopers say they have reported to accidents and sightings of the "Woman in White," who seems to wander on the narrow strip of pavement. A little girl has been seen playing in the vineyard on full moon nights, and a cowboy with his horse has literally walked through the walls of the processing building, causing the vineyard staff stress.

CLOUDCROFT

The small, picturesque mountain community of Cloudcroft, which means Cloud Pasture, celebrates being "nine thousand feet above stress level"—and they mean it. As you breathe in the crisp, cool air, you can feel your troubles melt away with every breath. Tall pines, quaint shops, fabulous barbecue and hamburgers, and, in some spots, beautiful views of the White Sands National Park in the Tularosa Basin below are what make this mountain community so attractive. It is located twenty miles east of Alamogordo, and the two towns as well as Carlsbad further south share a founding father, Charles Bishop Eddy, who was vital to bringing the railroad to these towns.

Forests surrounding the tent town of Cloudcroft were utilized for their "endless supply" of lumber for railroad timbers. Workers advised that the location would serve well as a tourist destination, and they were correct. Today, Cloudcroft provides the opportunity for many activities throughout the year, including ice skating, snow tubing, snow skiing, hiking, biking, and shopping. One activity that brings visitors to the Sacramento Mountain community is golf. The Lodge is home to a nine-hole regulation course that boasts a par of thirty-four with 2,387 total yardages. The course can be played twice to achieve a full eighteen holes. The first hole is a challenging 150-foot vertical drop to start your experience. It is proudly said to be one of North America's oldest golf courses since it was established in 1899, and for the first fifty years of its existence, one could say it was the highest course in North America as well. The four other courses now have this honor, but only by less than 600 feet, making the Lodge the fifth highest in North America at 9,000 feet.

The town holds several festivals each year, which bring a good number of tourists and locals to enjoy the festivities. As an artist community—and given the gorgeous scenery around the town, how could it not be? The arts and crafts fairs are next-level. Apples and cherries grow abundantly in the region, so there are also festivals to celebrate the harvests. Lumberjack Day will let you prove your prowess throwing an axe. Cloudcroft is also home to a herd of wild horses, so take care when you round the tight curves on the roads coming into town.

REBECCA'S AT THE LODGE
601 CORONA PLACE

An alpine-inspired hotel sits above Cloudcroft and plays host to travelers, businesspeople, and golfers from around the world. The Swiss chalet–style hotel resort features a tall tower, which can be accessed using an extremely narrow stairway; the views are worth the effort. The restaurant at the lodge is named in honor of a beautiful young woman named Rebecca Porter. You will notice many pieces of ephemera scattered throughout the lobby that tell her sad story, which we include in the following pages.

After beginning life as a headquarters for a logging camp in 1899, the lodge sadly burned to the ground, but luckily, it was rebuilt into the magical resort we know today. It opened again to the public in 1906, and the three-story Victorian we see today was completely rebuilt in 1911. Many famous guests have graced the threshold of the lodge, such as Judy Garland, Clark Gable, and even the Mexican revolutionary Francisco "Pancho" Villa. The lodge is also proud to say that every New Mexico territorial and state governor since 1901 has been their guest, and they have their very own Governor's Suite.

The impeccably manicured landscaping features huge pine and spruce trees. Light dances through the many intricate stained-glass windows in Rebecca's and scattered throughout the inn. Each room has its own theme and design. You can also enjoy outdoor dining, weather permitting; stroll through the garden; and play in the swimming pool in the summer months. Be sure to check out the basement bar called the Red Dog Saloon, which features live entertainment and dancing.

Haunted Tales

Chambermaid Rebecca is said to be a "friendly ghost," and in fact, her nature is what led her to become a spirit in the first place. While she was

The Lodge in Cloudcroft is one of the most beautiful examples of Alpine style in the state of New Mexico and features an observation tower.

working at the lodge (after it was rebuilt in the early 1920s), Rebecca's beauty was said to be hard to forget. The beauty with long, flaming red curls and blue eyes garnered a lot of attention, especially from the lumberjacks who were logging the area. The young woman lived in the basement rooms; her room was right behind the downstairs bathroom, alongside the rest of the employees, where the Red Dog Saloon is located today. This is one of Rebecca's favorite haunts, where she is sometimes seen dancing after hours.

One lumberjack allegedly claimed Rebecca for his own and became enraged when he witnessed the redhead in the arms of another man; she had taken on extracurricular activities in addition to her job as a maid. Unable to control his rage, the lumberjack is said to have dragged poor Rebecca into the surrounding woods, where he hacked her to death in a fit of rage and then disappeared. Reports also state the man receiving Rebecca's attention also disappeared around the same time.

Flickering lights, moving furniture, objects being moved, scraping sounds heard in the hallways, and fires igniting in some of the hotel fireplaces on their own have all been attributed to the playful ghost, who is often seen at the top of the stairs leading to the second floor. Rebecca seems partial to male guests and has been known to tickle their feet and whisper in their ears. Some accounts say Rebecca is buried on the lodge property, possibly on the golf course, and this may explain why she stays around the hotel.

Rebecca, who has been seen rearranging flowers in the various vases in the hallways, is not a frightening spirit, and guests often seek her out and invite interaction. Her alleged murderer, on the other hand, has also been sighted, but he is still in a rage and appears quite angry and threatening, invoking the opposite reaction. Luckily, he is not seen as often. Rebecca is said to be a playful prankster, but according to psychics, the apparition enjoys being at the lodge.

Other stories of ghostly encounters are told as well. A female guest who was in Room 104 with her husband woman awoke as the room had become warm and she felt a cold hand on her shoulder. What made this a bit creepy was that she reported a man singing the song "Won't You Be My True Love" in her ear. When she finally was able to move, she felt a cold gust of air, and the presence was gone. When the woman woke her husband, she found, to her frustration, that he had slept through the entire encounter.

In a separate room, a male guest saw a "vaporous female" waiting for him in the tub. Desk clerks have also witnessed a man dressed in an elegant tuxedo seat himself in Rebecca's, order two meals, and talk to someone in the chair facing him all night. The chair was completely empty, but both meal plates and wine glasses were empty by the end of the evening.

The forest surrounding the lodge is said to be a hotspot for paranormal activities. Ghost lights, which are atmospheric lights appearing without cause, and dancing orbs are observed in the meadows. Many reports of the elusive wendigo have also surfaced, causing great fright for those who state they have witnessed the tall, pale, bipedal antlered figure, a reportedly eight-foot-tall specter that towers over anyone who observes it.

But the most interesting reports are of those who swear they have seen up, close and personal, the equally elusive and bipedal Bigfoot. There have been many reports of sightings of Bigfoot from all over New Mexico. This hairy creature is generally seen in the northern mountains of New Mexico in the Jemez and Red River regions, but many sightings have also surfaced in Otero, Eddy, and Chaves Counties. These reports are studied by the Bigfoot Field Researchers Organization (BFRO), which keeps detailed documentation from witnesses. Could it be the lack of oxygen at high altitude causing hallucinations? The people reporting the sightings are quite varied and all seem genuine in their accounts.

CHAPTER 4
SOUTHWEST REGION

DEMING

Nestled in the southwestern corner of New Mexico, Deming is a highly agricultural region. Flanked by the Florida Mountains to the south and Las Cruces sixty miles away to the west, Deming is a centrally located spot on Interstate 10, also close to the Arizona border and thirty-three miles from Mexico. Rockhounds find the area especially alluring because of the existence of the Rockhound State Park, which features fire agates, thunder eggs, and crystal geodes. The City of Rocks State Park is in proximity as well. As this was a highly volcanic region, the geology is outstanding.

The area also seems to draw attention from the paranormal community. Like other cities in the state, it claims to be the most haunted city in New Mexico. Deming has seen much violence since its founding in 1881, given the Apache Wars involving Geronimo, Victorio, and Mangas Coloradas; its time as a center for healing for tuberculosis patients, who flocked west for the dry climate; and the multitudes of outlaws who roamed the expansive countryside.

There are many buildings in Deming that claim to be haunted besides the restaurants mentioned here, including the old jail, which once housed the Sheriff Dispatch Office; the Deming Luna Mimbres Museum; the Luna County Courthouse; and the Holy Cross Sanatorium, to name just a few. So, if you're looking for some other worldly activities, Deming is touted as an excellent place to hunt.

Above: Luna County Courthouse was the site of many public hangings because of Pancho Villa's invasion of the small community of Columbus.

Opposite: The New Mexico wine industry is supported heavily in Luna County as some of the oldest wineries are found in the shadow of the Florida Mountains.

The beautiful town of Deming is not all paranormal. Each year, it throws the Deming Duck Race, where over ten thousand people watch ducks of many sizes and shapes compete for their owners. The Les Combes Wine Fest is held in October to celebrate the wine harvest with wine and craft beer tasting and other activities. Be sure to go on a winery tour and participate in the grape-stomping and cork-pulling contests while you are there. The Luna Rossa Winery in Deming was largely responsible for saving the New Mexico wine industry when an unexpected late freeze occurred in the northern regions in the early 2000s, killing many of the vines in the state. Owners Paolo and Sylvia D'Andrea went above and beyond to help their fellow New Mexico winery owners.

For those of you who like things spicy, Deming offers the Salsa Festival Extravaganza, where you can taste some of the best salsas in the state and participate in jalapeño-eating contests if you are brave enough. If that's not

your speed, there are cornhole tournaments to help you digest the delicious chile, New Mexico's official state vegetable. Be sure to try the green chile while in southwestern New Mexico; they are famous for it there.

As you visit some of the haunted spots in Deming, be sure to cruise through town and see the stunning murals that are painted on the sides of the historic buildings. Huge clay pots adorned with Native American symbols are scattered throughout the town as well, especially at the downtown park with the fountain. Deming is worth the exit from Interstate 10.

ADOBE DELI
3970 LEWIS FLATS ROAD SE

Located approximately ten miles east of the town of Deming, New Mexico, the Adobe Deli sits by itself on the side of a narrow, partially paved road. A sign stating "Restaurant and Lounge" will be your first indication of the building's purpose. The restaurant's website touts the location as a "destination like no other," and they mean it. The Adobe Deli provides diners with a variety of choices for their dining experience. As a former schoolhouse for the village of Lewis Flats, the building has seen many phases in life since being built in 1936. It is said that one of the reasons

Once a schoolhouse, the Adobe Deli is home to a highly eclectic collection of lovingly curated antiques by the owner, Van Jacobson.

the schoolhouse closed was the high number of rattlesnakes that also liked to call the area home. The restaurant is located at the foot of the Florida Mountains, and the views are spectacular.

The deli has been owned since 1978 by New York native Van Jacobson, who, in his younger years, worked as a stage lighting expert for many famous bands of the 1970s. The purchase of the Adobe Deli was a stretch from the norm for him, but he has adapted well and provides a unique dining experience in the middle of the desert.

Everything about the Adobe Deli is unique. The location, décor, food, and owners make this out-of-the-way eatery a treasure for locals and tourists alike.

Haunted Tales

As a skeptic, Van Jacobson does not believe 100 percent in the presence of ghostly activity in his restaurant—even though he has had a particularly memorable experience himself. The story goes that Jacobson was making coffee one morning and spilled some on a countertop. After using a bar rag to clean it up, he found the words "Van dye" stained on the fabric. Still not phased but unable to explain, Jacobson admits it was odd, but he had too much work to do to worry about it.

Another story surrounding the Adobe Deli dates to 1980, when, during a dance to celebrate the town of Deming's centennial, a gentleman had a heart attack and died at the scene. The man's wife seemed to take it in stride; she was quoted saying, "He was having the best time of his entire life." Jacobson likes to think the man is still dancing.

Lewis Flats Memorial Cemetery is a short distance away from the Adobe Deli Restaurant and holds the well-cared-for graves of the pioneer Lewis family.

Although Jacobson is skeptical, his staff swear by their experiences, such as hearing faint piano music coming through the public address system as they are closing.

Travel Channel's *Ghost Adventures* visited the Adobe Deli in 2018 and had a few experiences; the team went as far as to say a portal exists in the cigar room of the restaurant. The show's stars were able to record disembodied voices, orbs, energy pulses, and even facial images—which they attributed to the large collection of Native and Old West artifacts adorning the walls of the entire restaurant. Although the owner is not a believer in ghosts, a paranormal group from nearby El Paso, Texas, also visited the Adobe Deli and was astounded by their findings. Ghostly figures were seen seated above the diners in a small false balcony area. Cold spots were abundant as were items moving without human help, and disembodied voices were caught on their equipment.

One cause of the restaurant haunting may be the small Lewis Flats Memorial Cemetery, which contains the graves of the Lewis pioneer family and is within eyeshot of the restaurant. It's possible these inhabitants feel a certain attraction to the building because of the number of artifacts there as well.

LAS CRUCES

Founded in 1849 after the Mexican American War, Las Cruces (The Crosses) has bragging rights for being the second-largest city in New Mexico. As a college town—home to New Mexico State University, which was founded in 1888 as the only land grant university in the state—Las Cruces has all the amenities necessary in a large city and is within thirty minutes of its sister city, El Paso, Texas.

Las Cruces has a rich ranching history and connections to the space program: the Spaceport America is only fifty-five miles away, in Truth or Consequences, the White Sands Missile Range, with its test range is at the base of San Augustine Pass, and there are several NASA facilities within the region. The city is well-versed in technology and agriculture. While in Las Cruces, visit the forty-seven-acre New Mexico Farm and Ranch Heritage Museum, which attracts many interesting exhibits throughout the year. As with most large towns in the state, the railroad played a huge role in its development. If a town got the railroad, it was through the luck of the draw; if it did not, most likely it is a ghost town today. The Las Cruces Railroad Museum holds the history of the rails for Las Cruces.

To the northeast of Las Cruces are the stunning Organ Mountains, which reach up to the sky like the organ pipes they were named for—except these needles are made of granite. These craggy mountains are part of the Rio Grande Rift Valley and, like the other mountain ranges in the state, were formed by violent volcanic activity. The Organ Mountains were made as a national monument in 2014 to protect over 496,000 thousand acres of precious land. This monument provides great opportunities for hiking, camping, and learning about the history of the region.

La Sierra De Los Órganos, or the Organ Mountains, were declared a national monument on May 21, 2014, and are located ten miles from Las Cruces.

MESILLA

Once occupied as the capital of the Confederate Territory of Arizona during the American Civil War, Mesilla has seen many occupations,: Native, Spanish, Mexican and Anglo. This type of occupation was experienced by most of the territory, which was one of the main reasons behind New Mexico not achieving statehood until 1912. Washington, D.C., was not positive where the loyalties of New Mexico's people lay since the state had been ruled under numerous flags.

Today, you will find the quaint village of Mesilla, only a five-minute drive from Las Cruces, to be a delight to visit. A central gazebo sets the stage for festivals, live music events, or a quick break from the New Mexico sun. The Mesilla Plaza, which has been a national landmark since 1961, is flanked by restaurants, bars, bookstores, and gift shops with thick adobe walls, which protected the original residents from the frequent raids by the Apache in the region. At the north end of the historic plaza sits the San Albino Church,

Mesilla, New Mexico, was the capital of the Confederate Territory of Arizona when it was occupied by Colonel John R. Baylor's troops in 1861.

which claims to be one of the oldest churches in the Mesilla Valley as it was constructed in 1851.

Mesilla Plaza is decorated with red chile ristras and paper flags, lending a festive atmosphere to the historical square. As you visit with the store owners and managers, you will hear wonderful stories about some of the characters who walked the narrow streets before you, characters such as boy bandit Billy the Kid, lawman Pat Garrett, outlaw gang leader John Kinney, and President Ulysses S. Grant, among many more.

DOUBLE EAGLE RESTAURANT/IMPERIAL BAR 2355 CALLE DE GUADALUPE

A one-thousand-pound gilded cast-iron post–American Civil War gate protects the magnificent adobe structure on the northeast corner of the Mesilla Plaza, which boasts one of the most widely known ghost stories of the Mesilla Valley and New Mexico as a whole: the ghostly lovers of the Double Eagle Restaurant. The opulently decorated restaurant boasts crystal chandeliers, gilded mirrors, rich tapestry, and old-world artwork as well as carpets and period furniture that once belonged to the Maes family, who originally owned this gorgeous property. Even the ceilings are impressive: The tin ceiling panels are accented with eighteen-karat gold.

Inside the Imperial Bar is a thirty-foot hand-carved Eastlake-style oak and walnut bar, which is elegantly flanked by four gold-leaf Corinthian columns, which instantly add to the ambiance. Not to be outdone by the bar, the bar lighting is spectacular as well: It features two five-foot Imperial French floral coronas adorned with twenty-three lighted brass flowers, of which ten feature exquisite Lalique blue crystal rosette shades. An antique brass footrail along the bottom of the wooden bar was obtained from the Billy the Kid Saloon—which was in what is now the Billy the Kid Gift Shop on the corner to the south of the Double Eagle Restaurant. The Imperial Bar is also festooned with two classic French Baccarat chandeliers, which measure seven feet by three feet in diameter. This room is certainly a feast for the eyes.

Built in 1849 as a private residence, the beautiful adobe structure is one of the oldest buildings on the Mesilla Plaza. Built around a central courtyard, the Double Eagle now features seven large dining rooms as well as the Imperial Bar. Each room is as elegantly adorned as the rest; you can never see everything in the rooms. You can dine in the Lew Wallace Room, named

A former palatial residence, the Double Eagle Restaurant is a cornerstone of the Mesilla Plaza and is steeped in rich history, mystery, and spirits.

after Governor Lew Wallace, author of *Ben Hur*; the Gadsden Room, which commemorates the signing of the Gadsden Purchase in the Mesilla Plaza; the Juarez-Diaz Room, named for the president of Mexico from 1876 to 1911 (this is now the entrance to the Peppers Restaurant, which is also a part of the Double Eagle Restaurant); the Carlotta Salon, the "ghost room" that used to serve as the bedroom of Armando Maes; the Maximillian Room, named for Ferdinand Maximillian Joseph, the archduke of Austria and emperor of Mexico, which is one of the most elaborately decorated rooms in the building; the Isabella Ballroom, which is named for Queen Isabella and holds the portrait of young Arabella, whom you will read about soon; and finally, the Billy the Kid Patio, named for New Mexico's most famous boy outlaw, William H. Bonney, also known as Billy the Kid. Included in the patio room is a carved newel post featuring his name and the name Maria from the home of Maria Gonzales in Lincoln, New Mexico; she was reported to be one of the Kid's many girlfriends.

Haunted Tales

Probably one of the most famous tales of any haunted restaurant is that of the murdered lovers of the Double Eagle Restaurant in Mesilla, which has been pieced together over the century since its occurrence through newspaper articles and old-timers' accounts.

The Maes (pronounced *Mays*) were a wealthy, extremely powerful Spanish family who liked to show off their wealth in their furnishings and surroundings, as evidenced by the restaurant today. Carlotta Maes had high hopes that her eldest son, Armando, would go forth and marry very well to continue the Maes lineage and wealth. She set her sights on an eligible family in Mexico City who had a daughter who fit the bill precisely to her liking and set forth plans to have the pair meet. It is not known if Armando was too keen on this arrangement, but it was the practice of the day.

Working for the family were many servants as it was a large home to maintain. One of the housemaids had a beautiful teenage daughter, Inez (sometimes spelled Ines), whom she would bring to work with her to help. Inez was told to stay away from the family, especially the young Maes son, but teenagers being teenagers, somehow the two managed to meet. Other household staff and, later, villagers knew about the two lovers' secrets and tried their best to conceal them, but Carlotta Maes noticed the flirtation between the young couple and immediately fired Inez and forbade her from entering the house from then on. The señora reminded her son of his obligation to the family and that he could not be seen with such a person of low quality; he was meant for aristocracy.

Not able to stay apart, the young lovers found a way to see each other in secret until Armando's mother returned home from a trip unexpectedly and found the pair in Armando's room in a compromising condition. Enraged by what she saw, Carlotta Maes stepped back in shock, went to her room, returned with a large pair of sharp sewing shears, and proceeded to stab Inez multiple times in a fit of rage.

To save Inez, Armando yelled, "No, Mama! No!" and placed himself between his raging mother and his lover, receiving fatal stab wounds in the back from his mother. A few accounts say Inez died that day and Armando died three days later in what is known as the Carlotta Salon of the Double Eagle Restaurant. Another account states Inez survived and was able to escape but succumbed to her wounds later. Either way, this was a tragedy that ended in two unnecessary deaths.

Carlotta Maes, it is said, was seemingly in a trance when she committed the stabbings, unable to focus during her rage, but when she heard her son's cries of pain and saw the shears in his back, the woman snapped back to reality. The scream Carlotta Maes released was one of complete horror and guttural pain. It is said Armando cradled the young Inez in his arms as she took her last breath and looked up into the corner, smiled, and went unconscious, only to die three days later. Villagers state "Armando" was the last word Carlotta Maes ever spoke from that day forward.

As ghosts, the teenage couple are known to be mostly pranksters: calling the names of staff members, moving silverware and chairs, and breaking wine glasses but nothing malicious. There are two upholstered chairs in the Carlotta Salon that no one is allowed to sit in—although they both show signs of wear on the arms and backs.

A young girl, whom restaurant staff call Arabella, is said to haunt the restaurant as well. A portrait of this forlorn little girl, about seven or eight years old, in a red dress with a doll can be seen in the Isabella Room. Legend says the face of the doll is the death mask of the little girl's mother. Whether this is true or not, the mother's face was painted on the doll in the painting as per the tradition of the time. Arabella likes to play under the tables and can be seen in the women's restroom and the hallway between the Isabella Room and the kitchen.

Another unnamed little girl, said to be Hispanic with long black hair, is also seen in the restaurant. When a medium visited the Double Eagle Restaurant, she stated this girl was somehow trapped there and could not leave. Could this be the same little girl who is seen laughing, giggling, and running through the Billy the Kid Gift Shop located at the other end of the same block? I say yes, as no walls can hold spirits and the descriptions match; she and Arabella are probably friends.

The alleged witch's grave is topped, ironically, with the largest iron cross in the center of the San Albino Cemetery, located just south of the Mesilla Plaza.

For those of you who are brave enough, there is a reported witch's grave in the San Albino Cemetery half a mile south of the Mesilla Plaza on Calle de Guadalupe. Legend states a local woman attempted to poison a man with a gift of a bowl of soup, but the man added some herbs and spices of his own and sent it back to the woman as a thank-you gift. The woman became very ill. When the woman later died, she was buried in the cemetery under a large rock to prevent her from rising out of her grave. This rock was then covered with concrete and topped with a tall metal cross. Interestingly, this is the largest grave in the cemetery.

Many of the surrounding residents believe the woman attempts to break free, so they make sure all cracks or holes that form on the base are fixed as soon as possible. As a result of the fixes, the base of the grave has become much larger than any other grave in the cemetery, although the maintenance has been somewhat lacking lately: The grave base has visible cracks. If you visit, a good cleanse is suggested.

La Posta de Mesilla 2410 Calle de San Albino

La Posta Restaurant, circa 1840, is a beautiful example of New Mexico architecture that graces the southeastern corner of the Mesilla Plaza. As a former trading post (hence the name La Posta) and stage stop for the Butterfield Stage Company, the sturdy walls of this historical building are made mainly of commonly used adobe bricks. Protection from the Apache was vital to survival in the mid-1800s. Built by brothers Roy and Sam Bean, of Texas Judge Roy Bean fame, it also housed the Corn Exchange Hotel for a decade between 1870 and 1880.

The owners of La Posta have in their possession old ledgers that show the names of those who passed through the doors in the early days when it was a hotel. One notable, President Ulysses S. Grant, stayed in the tiny outpost two times. Others include General Douglas MacArthur, Kit Carson, Pancho Villa, and William H. Bonney, also known as Billy the Kid.

La Posta de Mesilla—founded by Katherine "Katy" Griggs Camuñez, who is described as a true pioneer and renaissance woman—is a feast not only for the stomach, with its wonderful New Mexican cuisine, but for

La Posta De Mesilla has worn many hats over its lifetime and has played host to many dignitaries who traveled in the dangerous West.

the eyes as well. The restaurant is a fiesta of color, sights, and sounds. A large atrium is in the lobby, which contains many varieties of parrots and parakeets that provide a source of entertainment while one is waiting to be seated. Each section was once part of the original outpost, and the restaurant now encompasses the entire ten-thousand-square-foot building. The Tostadas Compuestas are considered the specialty of the house; pair them with a prickly pear margarita, and you are set for a fantastic meal experience.

Haunted Tales

One of the more commonly told stories about the hauntings at La Posta centers on the appearance of a little girl, six to eight years of age, who has been seen by staff members and restaurant patrons alike. How you experience her presence depends on your mood and openness of mind. Some say the little girl is fun and likes to play with restaurant staff and clients. This little girl is said to be connected to the family who once used the building as a private home before the additions.

Tales of the typical smashing glasses and moving chairs are told about La Posta, but so are stories of an obvious sulfuric smell and extreme temperature changes in the lobby/gift shop area of the restaurant. A presence is also said to disturb the parrots in the large aviary.

Women customers have said a man in a white shirt appears to be following them to the lobby or restroom, but when they turn around to confront him, he has vanished.

PIÑOS ALTOS

Piños Altos (Tall Pines in Spanish) was established when gold was discovered in Bear Creek by Robert "Three-Fingers" Birch, Colonel Jacob Snively, and James W. Hicks. The trio stopped to drink from the creek and were thrilled to see glints of gold at the bottom. A claim was quickly filed, and the mining boom town was born. The town was originally known as Birchville, named after the aforementioned Robert Henry Birch. Birch, a reformed outlaw, was dubbed the Banditti of the Prairie by author/detective Edward Bonney, who alleged Birch had connections with Tennessee outlaw John A. Murrell and his Mystic Clan when they committed murder and robbery in the Midwest. Birch died in the Arizona Territory in 1866.

In September 1861, Piños Altos was the site of the Battle of Piños Altos between the Arizona Guards (a Confederate Arizona Territorial militia), who occupied Piños Altos until 1862, and over four hundred Apache Warriors, Mangas Coloradas (also known as Red Sleeves), and Cochise, who were stirring up trouble for the incoming miners. During the first battle, several miners were killed, and the wooden buildings of the town were set on fire by the Natives while most of the militia were out on patrol. When they returned, the opposing sides exchanged gunfire for about two hours before the Natives made a huge final push.

Apache claims on the land went unheard. What the Natives saw as an invasion by the settlers and miners was the catalyst of their increased efforts to rid the land of the pests. This was the start of the Apache Wars, which brought death and destruction to both sides.

The turning point in the Battle of Piños Altos was brought on by a quick-thinking militia captain, who used an old cannon that sat in front of Roy (of Judge Roy Bean fame) and Sam Bean's store as an early version of an improvised explosive device, loading the barrel with rusty nails and buckshot to be shot toward the approaching tribe. The tactic worked: Many of the Natives were killed and others critically hurt, causing them to retreat. Violence continued to erupt for over a decade, and the groups took turns in outsmarting each other.

Using guerrilla tactics in the fight against the settlers, Mangas Coloradas was able to lure over forty miners to their deaths by staging a striptease done by Apache women on a hill. When the miners got closer for a better look, they were ambushed by the warriors. Mangas, who was said to be over seven feet tall, was invited to a friendly meeting by the residents of Birchville. When Mangas accepted, he was captured, tied to a tree, and whipped. The deaths of thirty or more Chiricahua Apache were attributed to an ambush by approximately thirty miners on the Mimbres River.

Mangas Coloradas's fate was set on January 17, 1863, when the aging leader came to Piños Altos to negotiate a petition for peace. He was met with disdain and immediately captured by the miners.

The disputes were not easily settled, and there were many deaths on both sides, necessitating the construction of Fort Bayard nearby in 1866 to protect the mining communities of the Black Range and Gila Mountain Regions, which allowed for mining to resume and development of the town

Fort Bayard was built to protect mining communities from the frequent attacks by local warring Indigenous tribes in the Black Range and Gila Mountains.

to continue. Sadly, the tall pines for which the town was named were cut down to build the necessary businesses and homes for nearly nine thousand residents in its heyday between 1880 and 1890.

BUCKHORN SALOON AND OPERA HOUSE
32 MAIN STREET

The exterior of the Buckhorn Saloon and Opera House looks much like it did when it was built in 1865. If you didn't know about the reputation of the cuisine and atmosphere available there, you might drive by a true gem of the Old West since the exterior, complete with hitching post, gives no hint of the wonders going on inside. Nestled in the heart of the mining ghost town of Piños Altos, eight miles north of Silver City, the restaurant, saloon, and opera house venue is the life of the one-street town and is quite popular with tourists and locals alike. Reservations are highly recommended as the dining rooms and bar fill up quickly.

Above: The stately Buckhorn Saloon and Opera House is the busiest place in Piños Altos on the weekends, serving delicious steaks and local fare.

Left: The Opera House is decorated in a luxurious Victorian style and harks back to the times when actors performed melodramas and tragedies onstage.

Known for its delicious steaks and varied cuisine, the Buckhorn sits 7,040 feet above sea level in the high desert environment of Piños Altos and must have been a raucous place back in the day as one of the eight saloons that graced the mountain community. Including many original and historic details, such as kiva fireplaces, Saltillo tile floors, vintage photographs, original artworks, and Old West artifacts, the restaurant, saloon, and adjoining opera house appear deceptively small from the outside. The saloon carries the distinction of being the oldest continually run saloon in the Southwest. They are decorated in a mixture of Southwestern and Victorian styles of the Old West, featuring both a gorgeous wooden mirrored back bar to greet you as you enter the Buckhorn Saloon and Opera House and stucco walls and kiva fireplaces as a homage to the Native and Southwestern influences in the region.

If you are in the Silver City area, a visit to the Buckhorn Saloon and Opera House is highly recommended. Come for the food and stay for the spirits.

Haunted Tales

Showing up unannounced at the Buckhorn early one afternoon to see if I could make a dinner reservation early, I was thrilled to be given a personal tour of the historic building by the extremely knowledgeable manager, Katie Alecksen, who, at the time, had been working there for seven years. Katie was kind enough to relay some fascinating ghost stories to me, for which I am beyond grateful.

Since Katie has worked in the building for so long, odd occurrences do not seem to faze her; she smiles and says it's all in a day's work. Katie stated she wasn't sure if one event she experienced could be considered paranormal activity, but it was certainly strange. After spending the better part of the day cleaning the entire front bar area, where a figure in a cowboy hat had previously been seen, Katie finished and sat down for some much-needed rest. Just as she did so, a full bottle of Johnny Walker Black exploded on the bar back, spewing its contents over all her hard work. No one was in the room but her at the time.

At the Opera House bar, which is in the back portion of Buckhorn, bar glasses are known to frequently fly off the end of the bar without provocation. Attempts to debunk this activity have been made by staff and patrons alike

Private viewing theater boxes line the walls of the Opera House, where elegantly dressed apparitions have been reportedly seen by the hired stage performers.

by adding water or ice to the bar top and glass bottom, but no one has been able to replicate the activity. As soon as their efforts cease, another glass goes flying. The aroma of cigar smoke is often reported around this bar top as well, although there is no smoking allowed in the building.

A couple taking a selfie video at this bar reported recording a shadowy figure in the mirror behind the bar walking by as they were shooting. Doors also are reported to close by themselves in rooms without drafts and no one present.

Live entertainment is brought into the Buckhorn Saloon and Opera House on a weekly basis and for special occasions. On one such occasion, known as the Winter Ball, which is held each February, a band was set up on the stage toward the back of the room. Since this is the event of the year, everyone from Piños Altos, Silver City, and the surrounding towns came to the Buckhorn dressed to the nines in formal wear. A live band is hired each year to add to the festivities. Katie reported that one of the band members told her it was a nice touch having people in period clothing in the elevated boxes around the room. The only problem was, the Buckhorn had not done anything of the sort.

One other reason for the large number of hauntings in the building may be an awful incident that occurred after the Battle of Piños Altos. A peace treaty was finally drafted between the warring factions to stop the constant attacks from the two sides. A dinner to celebrate the treaty signing in the Buckhorn Saloon and Opera House building was interrupted by a settler who opened gunfire on the party attendees, including sixty unarmed Natives. Many of the Natives were killed and wounded, thus extending the war for many more years—possibly even till today.

BIBLIOGRAPHY

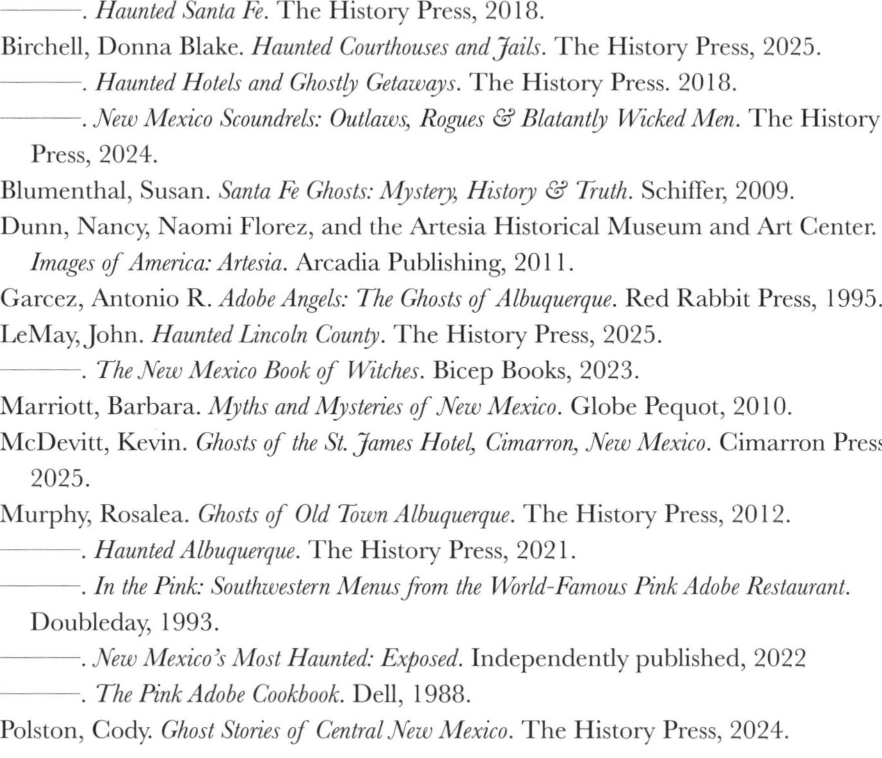

Aragon, Ray John de. *Enchanted Legends and Lore of New Mexico: Witches, Ghosts & Spirits*. The History Press, 2012.

———. *Haunted Santa Fe*. The History Press, 2018.

Birchell, Donna Blake. *Haunted Courthouses and Jails*. The History Press, 2025.

———. *Haunted Hotels and Ghostly Getaways*. The History Press. 2018.

———. *New Mexico Scoundrels: Outlaws, Rogues & Blatantly Wicked Men*. The History Press, 2024.

Blumenthal, Susan. *Santa Fe Ghosts: Mystery, History & Truth*. Schiffer, 2009.

Dunn, Nancy, Naomi Florez, and the Artesia Historical Museum and Art Center. *Images of America: Artesia*. Arcadia Publishing, 2011.

Garcez, Antonio R. *Adobe Angels: The Ghosts of Albuquerque*. Red Rabbit Press, 1995.

LeMay, John. *Haunted Lincoln County*. The History Press, 2025.

———. *The New Mexico Book of Witches*. Bicep Books, 2023.

Marriott, Barbara. *Myths and Mysteries of New Mexico*. Globe Pequot, 2010.

McDevitt, Kevin. *Ghosts of the St. James Hotel, Cimarron, New Mexico*. Cimarron Press, 2025.

Murphy, Rosalea. *Ghosts of Old Town Albuquerque*. The History Press, 2012.

———. *Haunted Albuquerque*. The History Press, 2021.

———. *In the Pink: Southwestern Menus from the World-Famous Pink Adobe Restaurant*. Doubleday, 1993.

———. *New Mexico's Most Haunted: Exposed*. Independently published, 2022

———. *The Pink Adobe Cookbook*. Dell, 1988.

Polston, Cody. *Ghost Stories of Central New Mexico*. The History Press, 2024.

Radford, Benjamin. *Mysterious New Mexico: Miracles, Magic and Monsters in the Land of Enchantment*. University of New Mexico Press, 2014.

Ravencrest, Devon. *Albuquerque Spirits: The Ultimate Guide to Spine-Chilling Legends in New Mexico's Haunted Restaurants, Bars, and Hotels*. Independently published, 2024.

Rogal, Christine. *Haunted New Mexico: Ghosts and Strange Phenomena of the Land of Enchantment*. Globe Pequot, 2021.

INDEX

D

E

F

G

H

About the Author

Exploring her home state of New Mexico is author Donna Blake Birchell's favorite pastime. Sharing what she has found gives her great joy, and she hopes you will find as much enjoyment in your own treks of discovery in the Land of Enchantment.

Visit us at
www.historypress.com